D1498581

LATINO U.S.A.:
A CARTOON HISTORY

Also by **Ilan Stavans** in English

Fiction
The One-Handed Pianist and Other Stories

Nonfiction
The Riddle of Cantinflas
Art and Anger
The Hispanic Condition
Bandido
Imagining Columbus

Anthologies
The Oxford Book of Jewish Stories
The Urban Muse
New World
Mutual Impressions
The Oxford Book of Latin American Essays
Tropical Synagogues
Growing Up Latino

Translations
Sentimental Songs, by Felipe Alfau

General
The Essential Ilan Stavans

LATINO U.S.A.: A CARTOON HISTORY

BY ILAN STAVANS

ILLUSTRATED BY LALO ALCARAZ

BASIC BOOKS

A Member of the Perseus Books Group

Produced by the Philip Lief Group

TO MY STUDENTS AT AMHERST COLLEGE

Copyright © 2000 by The Philip Lief Group, Inc. and Ilan Stavans

Published by Basic Books,
A Member of the Perseus Books Group

Produced by the Philip Lief Group, Inc.
A CIP catalog record for this book is available from the Library of Congress.
ISBN-13 978-0-465-08221-6 ISBN-10 0-465-08221-1
First Edition

DHSB   12 11 10 9 8 7

Contents

PART 2: INTO THE CAULDRON: 1891-1957   43

FOREWORD

¡¡¡Splash!!! ¡¡¡Kaboom!!! Ay diosito, y ahora, ¿quién nos salvará?
-Kalimán: El hombre increíble

Pop art, the highbrows say, is junk. It results, so the argument goes, from the masses wanting to satisfy their spiritual thirst without any sense of refinement. Pure art is the result of an artist's finding an aesthetic way to channel his purposeful alienation from society into an original and authentic creation. But pop art—in German, *kitsch*— is art by imitation: second-rate, derivative, a hand-me-down. It does not come about out of inspiration but is assembled, manufactured, and thus, has no soul to speak of.

The problem with this view, of course, is that it is utterly false, to say nothing of snobbish and supercilious. If everything popular is by definition unworthy and inadequate, then all modernity, from beginning to end, is counterfeit, particularly in the vast regions of the globe where Europe was for endless years the sole provider of so-called legitimate art.

I came of age in Mexico, in the 1970s, surrounded by fast food, American TV sitcoms, cartoons, and Muzak. "Is there a true national art?" asked the intellectuals, distressed by the prevailing "colonial" mentality. The United States is nothing but artificial, they claimed, looking instead to Mexico's rich past. Why, then, I might have retorted, does the country need so much trash to survive? Why is *Star Wars* so popular? Furthermore, why is pop art in Mexico—soaps, comic strips, rock music—so deceptive? They would point at muralists Diego Rivera and Frida Kahlo, musicians Carlos Chávez and Silvestre Revueltas, litterateurs Ramón López Velarde, and Alfonso Reyes as models to emulate.

I was overexposed to this "illiteracy," this bastard nature of pop art, which supposedly underlined the abysmal ignorance of the masses. All kitsch is pernicious, but Mexican kitsch is twice as bad, for it is derived from an already derivative product—a Xerox of a Xerox. Nothing in this argument made sense to me. I loved Indiana Jones, ate burritos at Taco Bell, watched episode after episode of *Simplemente María*, listened to Juan Gabriel, and voraciously read the strips El Payo, Kalimán, and *Los supermachos*. My feeling, had I been asked, was that the authenticity of it all was found precisely in its beautiful unoriginality. Pop culture, my instinct told me, was much closer to the nation's collective psyche than anything by Kahlo and Reyes.

Comic strips and cartoons were my favorite pastime. They were known invariably as *los monitos, los comics, las tiras*. I dreamed, from early on, of becoming first a graphic artist and then a filmmaker. I was held spellbound by the union of word and image. A baroque kiosk just a few blocks from my house festively displayed all sorts of comic books. I found in them, and my friends did too, a much-needed dose of adventure, laughter, and satire. Poetic language, Aristotelian unity, intellectual sophistication, these were alien terms to me. What I wanted most was salvation through escape to become a superhero—*a la mexicana*—part mariachi and part Spiderman, to ridicule the ruling political elite, to travel to the Chiapas rainforest by horse with a flamboyant maid by my side. A cheap imagination? Well, perhaps, but vivid nonetheless. TV and comics were not noxious. I found them electrifying.

Mine was not an escapist middle-class mentality, as I have often heard it described. Mexico's population in its entirety, men and women, children and adults, rich and poor, rulers and the populace, also visited the kiosk, delivering the rigorous 3.50 pesos without any misgivings whatsoever. Paul Theroux, in his 1979 travelogue *The Old Patagonian Express*, writes that, arriving in San Luis Potosí, "I went to the plaza and bought a Mexican newspaper... the rest of the [train] passengers bought comic books." The division between haves and have-nots is clear, Theroux being among the latter. I can hardly invoke, as I look back, a more egalitarian pastime, one as democratic in its mission. And things have hardly changed since I grew up and since Theroux visited Mexico. Just ask any street vendor to describe who the audience for comics really is: todo el mundo, he will automatically say, just about everybody. A few comics were imports badly translated into Spanish, but most of the ones I read were not. They proudly displayed the logo *Hecho en México*, certifying not only that they were written, designed, and produced by nationals, but that nationals, too, consumed them en masse.

I am aware of the argument, defended most prominently by Irene Herner, and by Ariel Dorfman with Armand Mattelart in their book *How to Read Donald Duck*, that, in the so-called Third World, the comics industry is linked to American imperialism. Walt Disney's characters, so the litany goes, are hardly about innocence. Their tainted message is designed "to colonize the minds of children all over Latin America." Nonsense, I say, *puras tonterías*. Our global culture is not about exclusion and isolation, but about cosmopolitanism, which, etymologically, derives from the Greek terms *cosmos* and *polis*, a planetary city.

My strip heroes were definitely locals. Kalimán, among them, an immensely handsome, intellectually portentous macho, defied stereotypes. Raised by Tibetan monks, his mission is to ensure the security of the earth, not just Mexico, through his astonishing breadth of knowledge and enviable bodily strength. Who ever said Mexicans are dumb and without role models? Blue-eyed, uncorrupted, generous, he was much like Borges's Funes the Memorious: he spoke all human languages, was a walking encyclopedia, and even communicated with animals. These attributes were sustained by daily yoga exercises, meditation, and physical relaxation. Batman and Superman, Kalimán's role models, in my eyes seemed to pale when compared to him.

Equally compelling were other superheroes of more indigenous breeds, such as El Zorro and El Payo, the former a mestizo in nineteenth-century New Mexico, the latter a charro with an admirable sense of righteousness. Or El Santo, a masked wrestler. Or Chanoc himself, a Mayan ace raised in Ixtac, on the southern coast of Mexico, whose portentous swimming habits and expertise with knives allow him to kill one gigantic animal after another. Or some more prosaic quadruped, like Paquín and El Chamaco, Rocambole, Memín and Detective Fisgón, Adelita and Condorito. Sure, they are all manipulative, repetitive, and predictable. But they were a source of national pride, too. How many enjoyable school-bus rides did we spend together? How often did I hide them inside a history textbook, trusting they could offer a better lesson in civics?

Unlike elitist art, comics, although not quite anonymous, pay little attention to ownership. An author's name, with very few exceptions, is invisible. One of the exceptions is Eduardo del Río, aka Rius, probably the most prolific, versatile, and personal of Mexico's cartoonists. Born in 1935 in Zamora, Michoacán, he went to school in the nation's capital and, before becoming a national figure, he worked in a bar, a bottling plant, a funeral parlor, and as a delivery boy in a firm that distributed Walt Disney's comics. He began working as a cartoonist for various newspapers until, switching to comic strips, he produced *Los supermachos*, a political satire that, in the late 1960s, attacked President Gustavo Díaz Ordaz. It was adapted to theater and made into a film, *Calzonsin Inspector*, by Alfonso Arau, famous as the director of *Like Water for Chocolate*. Rius ran into trouble with the government for his strong Marxist views. He was fired and rehired elsewhere. Eventually he managed to build his own one-man company, which produced another landmark film, *Los agachados*.

Ideology, obviously, is at the core of his art. His characters are social types, archetypes, and stereotypes. His style, displayed in some 2,000 original fouilletons and booklets, most notably *Cuba Libre* and *El amor en los tiempos del Sida*, is not quite what strip readers are used to. Instead of developing a plot, he often explores national and international issues by dropping capsules of commentary that mix information with humor. He pioneered this didactic approach in *Marx for Beginners* and *The Myth of the Virgin of Guadalupe*, which are available in English, too.

(I stopped reading Rius one specific day, when a most anti-Semitic installment of *Los agachados*, endorsing Hitler, reached my hand. I have kept the strip with me, a testament to my disillusion.)

I came to learn that there are more comic strip publishers in Mexico than in any other Latin American country by far and I had also witnessed the boom of Mexican comics. Individual weekly issues had print runs varying between 300,000 and almost 9 million copies, by all accounts an astronomical number, particularly when compared to the Lilliputian number of books sold by literary figures. For example, books by authors of the stature of Carlos Fuentes often sold fewer than 10,000 copies per title in half a decade. And this huge number of comics didn't include exports to Central or South America and especially to areas of the United States highly populated with Latin Americans: East Los Angeles, Chicago's Pilsen and La Villita, and San Francisco's Mission District. *¡Jijole!*, El Chamaco would say.

The true roots of the strips, these "filthy artifacts," as arrogant intellectuals called them, are much contested in the artistic and academic communities. Some attribute the inspiration to Egyptian hieroglyphics and perhaps to illuminated Medieval manuscripts. Some even claim Aztec codices, ancient writings, and other pre-Columbian images as the true sources of Mexican comics. While I agree some inspiration may have been drawn from the Aztecs and other pre-Columbian societies, I believe that the strips have the exact same inspiration that nurtured the highbrow yet populist art of Rivera and Kahlo—the *retablos*, anonymous paintings that include a written prayer, which were offered by Catholic believers to Jesus Christ and the Virgin de Guadalupe as a token of appreciation for a miracle performed. I also believe the cartoonists drew inspiration from the engravings and pennydreadfuls (sensationalist writings of crime or violent adventure) of lampoonist José Guadalupe Posada. Posada invented the *calavera*, a skeleton poking fun at death and destiny that, with time, has come to represent for Mexico what Uncle Sam does for the United States.

I remember studying many a calavera with scrupulous eyes. What did I see? Myself? The histrionics of those around me? A perfect mask, no doubt. Masks, indeed, are what Mexican pop culture are all about: faces hidden behind faces. The Mexican shuts himself from the world, wrote Octavio Paz. "In his harsh solitude, which is both barbed and courteous, everything serves him as a defense: silence and words, politeness and disdain, irony and resignation." What Posada did so well, and modern strips continue doing, is to exploit, effortlessly, the smile behind those masks.

This passion for graphic art, for using images as vehicles of communication, is not accidental. It is inherent to Mexican culture, whereas the written word is, in many ways, an imported property. The way the Mexicans have turned words into a communication tool, both in conjunction with graphic images and alone, however, is astonishing.

As I matured, I came to realize the whole Hispanic world was home to millions of comic strips. My cadre of idols grew dramatically. From Posada and Rius, I graduated to Abel Quezada, whose endearing work was featured in *The New Yorker* in the 1980s. I then found my all-time favorite, Quino, the nom de plume of Joaquín Lavado, the Argentinean artist responsible for creating the character of Mafalda, a little girl whose sharpness and wisdom make her readers realize how convoluted our modern times are. ("Please stop the world!" she screams in a strip, "I want to get off!") I soon appreciated the deftness and flair with which

Fernando Botero, the master Colombian painter, turned cartoons into highbrow art. This led me to realize how fragile the line is between avant-garde and "junk." By the time I settled in the United States, graffiti and the Chicano cartoons and murals in California by Frank Romero and Ester Hernández had become a magnet, for what is street art if not the attempt to return iconography to the masses?

As Hispanics—a large majority of them Mexicans—cross the Rio Grande to become Latinos, they might switch languages, but their joie de vivre remains intact. I myself have always been fascinated by the challenges of capturing the joys, nuances, and multiple dimensions of Latino culture within the context of the English language. Hence, when a phone call from Sheila Friedling, an old friend and editor of an early book of mine, came with the invitation to do a cartoon history of Latinos, I was enthralled. Long-dormant adolescent memories surfaced, and Rius's art flashed into my mind. I also thought of a favorite experimental book I once read, *Fantomas contra los vampiros multinacionales* by Julio Cortázar, and fruitlessly looked for my old copy. Cortázar appropriated the character of the legendary French thief Fantomas, a Robin Hood of sorts, to ruminate, through cartoons, against U.S. imperialism. It surely was not the most inspired performance by the author of *Hopscotch*, but it was unquestionably an endearing tryout. And I reread *Cosmicomics* too, a fin-de-siècle novel by Italo Calvino, inspired by comics inspired by novels. I even asked myself: When did I really become a writer? Was it by reading one too many installments of *Los supermachos* or when I finished *Don Quixote*, fully hypnotized by its magic? The opportunity had arrived to become, finally, a manufacturer of kitsch, while paying tribute to a core aspect of my upbringing that I had cast aside when I focused my professional career on the muses of literature and academia.

In developing the manuscript for *Latino U.S.A.: A Cartoon History*, I consciously sought to combine the solemnity of so-called serious literature and history with the inherently theatrical and humorous nature of the comics. The experience was liberating: as an essayist, I am handcuffed by the abstraction of words, by the merciless need to make a cohesive, persuasive argument with words only. Cartoons and comics present the perfect stage to blend words and images, and engage the reader with their freshness, imagination, caricatures, and fantastical and delightfully irreverent overtones. Naturally thespian in their format, with characters spouting lines against an ever-changing backdrop of realistic and exaggerated settings, cartoons and comics can be more anarchic than a typical drama. My models from the theatrical world were Cervantes and

Rius, Pirandello, and Chanoc... as imagined by Mafalda.

My objective was to represent Hispanic civilization as a fiesta of types, archetypes, and stereotypes. As soon as I began sketching the layout, Posada's calaveras took control of me, as did other cliche figurines: a toucan, displayed regularly in books by Gabriel García Márquez, Isabel Allende, and the like; a beautiful señorita, addressing the exuberant sexuality I grew up with; Cantinflas, a beloved comedian known, paradoxically, as "the Hispanic Charlie Chaplin" (even after Chaplin described himself as "second best to Cantinflas"); a masked wrestler; and so on. By featuring these strips as the narrators and counternarrators of their own history and as actors on an imaginary stage, I avoided using, as much as possible, an official, impartial tone, embracing instead the rhythms of carnival. My "unofficialness" translated itself into what I think is a less Europeanized, more democratic viewpoint. History, of course, is a kaleidoscope where nothing is absolute. The human past and present are far more malleable than the future. This, in short, is my own account, a pastiche of angles I have made my own.

Matching with cartoonist Lalo López Alcaraz was the key relationship that shaped the vision, humor, and form of the book. Ever since I came across his cartoon La Cucaracha in *LA Weekly* and read *Pocho*, his satirical Chicano magazine, I realized I had found my artistic soulmate. I was born in Distrito Federal, he in San Diego: between the two of us, I trust, we are able to capture the perspectives of both south and north of the Rio Grande; also, both of us are fluent in Spanish and English with a fascination with Spanglish, the new integration of these two languages. His strips are about mischief and caprice, poking fun at human nature without compromising historical integrity. I trust his strips and my ideas are complementary echoes, echoooooooes. . . Everything in them is purposeful imitation.

—Ilan Stavans

AMERICA, AMERICA...

SWEET LAND OF LIBERTY! BUT THE WORD ALSO REFERS TO THE ENTIRE LANDMASS FROM ALASKA TO THE PATAGONIA.

YOU SAY GRANDE AND I SAY BRAVO... I SAY POTATO AND YOU SAY PO-TAH-TOE. GRANDE, BRAVO POTATO, PO-TAH-TOE LET'S CALL THE WHOLE THING OFF...

BROWNSVILLE

CIUDAD JUAREZ

WELCOME TO EL OTRO LADO

AMERICA THE NATION AND AMERICA THE CONTINENT.

THE RIVER MARKING THE BORDER BETWEEN MEXICO AND THE UNITED STATES IS 1,800 MILES LONG, AND IS KNOWN TODAY BY TWO NAMES: IF YOU STAND IN CIUDAD JUAREZ, ARE A SPANISH SPEAKER AND LOOK NORTH, IT IS THE RIO BRAVO -THE BRAVE RIVER, BUT IF YOU STAND IN BROWNSVILLE, SPEAK ENGLISH, AND LOOK SOUTH IT'S THE RIO GRANDE- THE BIG RIVER.

NO DOUBT THE FIRST STEP TO LEARNING LATINO HISTORY IS LEARNING THE RIVER'S NAME, BUT PEOPLE CAN'T MAKE UP THEIR MIND AS TO WHICH SINGLE NAME TO USE, AND YOU KNOW WHY? BECAUSE THE RIVER IS MUCH MORE THAN A SIMPLE RIVER, IT IS ALSO A BOUNDARY SEPARATING TWO OPPOSING WORLD VIEWS...

4

RIO GRANDE

N

SINCE THIS BOOK IS IN ENGLISH, I SUGGEST CALLING THE BORDER THE **RIO GRANDE.** WHAT DO YOU SAY?

AS YOU WISH, AMIGA. I SUGGEST YOU NOTIFY THE AUTHOR RIGHT AWAY TO AVOID CONFUSION.

THE RIO GRANDE IS WHERE LATIN AMERICA ENDS AND THE UNITED STATES BEGINS

YOU ARE NOW ILLEGALLY ENTERING THE **USA**

ORIS THAT THE OTHER WAY AROUND?

YO TENGO MIEDO, NO HABLO INGLES.

I GUESS YOU GUYS WILL BE NEEDING SOME ENGLISH LESSONS.

COYOTE

YO HABLO QUECHUA Y UN POCO DE ESPAÑOL.

PERU

THE HISTORY OF LATINOS IS THE HISTORY OF THE CLASH OF LANGUAGES—ENGLISH AND SPANISH—AND OF CULTURES—ANGLO-SAXON AND HISPANIC. THE TERM **HISPANIC** IS USED OUTSIDE THE UNITED STATES TO DESCRIBE THE CULTURES THAT DEVELOPED AS A RESULT OF SPANISH EXPLORATION, IN AND AFTER 1492, WHEN CHRISTOPHER COLUMBUS FIRST SET FOOT IN THE BAHAMAS AND CENTRAL AMERICA. **IBERIA** WAS THE NAME THE GREEKS USED FOR SPAIN, THE ROMANS CALLED IT **ESPERIA.**

6

LATINOS ARE A GROUP MADE OF MANY SUBGROUPS. THE U.S. CENSUS BUREAU HAS ESTABLISHED THAT THERE ARE AROUND 70 DIFFERENT VARIATIONS OF LATINOS DEPENDING ON THEIR RACE, GENDER, LANGUAGE, COUNTRY OF ORIGIN, etc. THE 1990 CENSUS COUNTED A TOTAL OF 25 MILLION, BUT THAT IS WITHOUT THE <u>INDOCUMENTADOS</u>.

THAT IS, ALIENS WITHOUT LEGAL DOCUMENTS.

"ALIEN," I HATE THE WORD. WHAT ARE LATINOS, EXTRA-TERRESTRIAL?

BY THE YEAR **2025** LATINOS WILL NUMBER ALMOST 50 MILLION, THE LARGEST MINORITY GROUP IN THE UNITED STATES.

LATINOS 23%
WHITES 29%
OTHER 10%
BLACKS 17%
ASIANS 21%

THE WHOLE ENCHILADA

9

MOST LATINOS ARE OF MEXICAN DESCENT AND THEY GO BY DIFFERENT NAMES: CHICANOS, MEXICANOS, MEXICAN-AMERICANS, MEX-AMERICANS, OR LA RAZA. THEY CONSTITUTE THE LARGEST SUB-GROUP WITHIN THE LATINO POPULACE, ABOUT 62 PERCENT. THE OTHER TWO MAJOR SUB-GROUPS ARE CUBANS AND PUERTO RICANS. THE LAST SUB-GROUP IS MADE OF OTHER NATIONALS: SALVADORANS, COLOMBIANS, DOMINICANS, NICARAGUANS AND OTHER LATINOS.

MEXICAN-AMERICANS

PUERTO RICANS

CUBAN-AMERICANS

OTHER LATINOS

CENTRAL AMERICANS

AND THEY EACH HAVE THEIR OWN "CAPITAL" WITHIN THE U.S.: MOST CHICANOS LIVE IN LOS ANGELES AND THE SURROUNDING AREAS, MOST CUBANS IN MIAMI, AND MOST PUERTO RICANS IN NEW YORK.

BUT GO TO LA VILLITA IN CHICAGO AND NOTICE HOW ALIVE MEXICAN CULTURE CAN BE IN THE WINDY CITY. OR ENJOY CUBAN CUISINE IN PATTER-SON, NEW JERSEY.

14

ALVAR NÚÑEZ CABEZA DE VACA IS THE AUTHOR OF THE FIRST MAJOR NARRATIVE OF EXPLORATION OF NORTH AMERICA. A FORTUNE HUNTER AND SPANISH NOBLEMAN, HE WAS THE TREASURER OF A SPANISH EXPEDITION, LED BY PÁNFILO DE NARVÁEZ. THIS EXPEDITION CLAIMED FOR THE SPANISH CROWN A VAST AREA, INCLUDING TERRITORY THAT IS NOW FLORIDA, LOUISIANA AND TEXAS.

BUT CABEZA de VACA'S JOURNEY WAS NOT QUITE HEROIC.

"HISPANIOLA"
MÉXICO
FLORIDA

IN FACT, IT WAS ONE MISADVENTURE AFTER ANOTHER. CABEZA DE VACA SUFFERED A SHIPWRECK, AND, WITH A HANDFUL OF MEN, WAS FORCED TO MAKE A LONG JOURNEY TO THE WEST, JOINING INDIAN TRIBES, LEARNING THEIR LANGUAGES AND CUSTOMS.

TO SURVIVE, HE OFTEN PRETENDED TO BE A PHYSICIAN OR MAGICIAN, DEPENDING ON THE CIRCUMSTANCE. HE ENDED UP A SLAVE MORE THAN ONCE. IN THE END HE MOVED TO MEXICO WHERE HE MET CORTÉS.

BOOK SIGNING TODAY "SHIPWRECK" MEET THE AUTHOR "WRONG WAY" CABEZA de VACA

SHIPWRECK
SHIPWRECK

BOOK SIGNING TODAY CABEZA de VACA

A BAD BOOK IF I MAY SAY SO!

HIS JOURNEY IS DESCRIBED IN THE BOOK **SHIPWRECK**.

CABEZA DE VACA WASN'T A WRITER, HE WAS JUST A SOLDIER WHO SPENT EIGHT YEARS—FROM 1528 TO 1536—TOTALLY LOST.

YES, HE WAS THE FIRST LATINO TO BE LOST... THIS REMINDS ME OF THE FAMOUS AMERICAN SPIRITUAL:

AMAZING GRACE

HOW SWEET
THE SOUND
THAT SAVED
A WRETCH
LIKE ME
I ONCE WAS LOST
BUT NOW AM FOUND
WAS BLIND
BUT NOW I SEE

A SPIRITUAL THAT BELONGS TO ALL OF US. AMONG MEXICAN-AMERICANS, A CORRIDO TELLS A SIMILAR THEME.

QUE TRISTE SE
ENCUENTRA EL HOMBRE
CUANDO ANDA AUSENTE
CUANDO ANDA AUSENTE
ALLA LEJOS DE SU PATRIA.
PIORMENTE SI SE ACUERDA
DE SUS PADRES Y SU CHATA
¡AY QUE DESTINO!
PARA SENTARME
A LLORAR.

TO BE LOST... AH, WHAT AN UNFORTUNATE AND ALL TOO COMMON OCCURRENCE.

"The Indians I found run with firebrands in their hands, burning the woods and fields they encounter, both to drive away the mosquitoes and force lizards and other similar animals out of the ground, to eat them. They kill deer too by surrounding them with many fires."

CABEZA DE VACA'S DESCRIPTIONS OF THE NATIVES AND OF NATURE IN THE AMERICAS IS SO DISTORTED. IT'S THE WAY EUROPEANS ALWAYS WANTED TO SEE THESE LANDS - MAGICAL, EXOTIC, FILLED WITH PRIMITIVE UNCIVILIZED PEOPLE. IT WOULD TAKE CENTURIES TO OVERCOME THESE MISCONCEPTIONS.

MANY OTHER **EXPLORERS** AND **CHRONICLERS**, EVEN POETS, SEARCHED FOR AND DESCRIBED THE TERRITORIES IN WHAT IS TODAY THE SOUTHWEST. AMONG THE MOST IMPORTANT WAS **FRANCISCO VÁZQUEZ DE CORONADO**, WHO BETWEEN 1540 AND 1542 LED A SPANISH EXPEDITION FROM **ARIZONA** TO **OKLAHOMA** AND **KANSAS**. THROUGHOUT THE 16th AND UP UNTIL THE 17th CENTURY, THE ONLY HISTORICAL ACCOUNTS WE HAVE OF WHAT LATINOS WOULD ONE DAY BECOME ARE BY SPANIARDS, <u>CRIOLLOS</u> AND <u>MESTIZOS</u> IN SPAIN AND IN MEXICO.

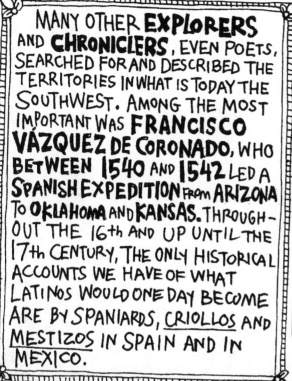

CRIOLLOS WERE SPANIARDS BORN IN THE NEW WORLD. MESTIZOS WERE PEOPLE OF MIXED RACE, PART SPANISH AND PART INDIAN.

NEW SPAIN, THAT'S WHAT MEXICO WAS CALLED DURING COLONIAL TIMES.

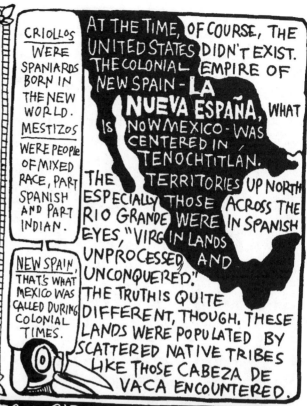

AT THE TIME, OF COURSE, THE UNITED STATES DIDN'T EXIST. THE COLONIAL EMPIRE OF NEW SPAIN - **LA NUEVA ESPAÑA**, WHAT IS NOW MEXICO - WAS CENTERED IN TENOCHTITLÁN. TERRITORIES UP NORTH ACROSS THE RIO GRANDE WERE IN SPANISH EYES, "VIRGIN LANDS UNPROCESSED, AND UNCONQUERED." THE ESPECIALLY THOSE THE TRUTH IS QUITE DIFFERENT, THOUGH. THESE LANDS WERE POPULATED BY SCATTERED NATIVE TRIBES LIKE THOSE CABEZA DE VACA ENCOUNTERED.

THE FAMOUS MYTH OF THE SEVEN CITIES OF CIBOLA LED MANY TO BELIEVE THAT THERE WAS ENORMOUS WEALTH IN THESE LANDS.

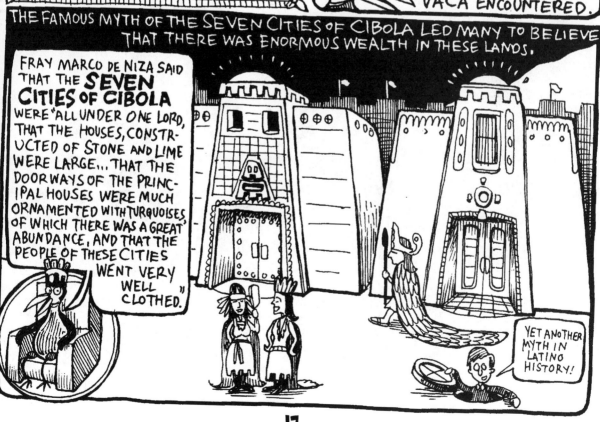

FRAY MARCO DE NIZA SAID THAT THE **SEVEN CITIES OF CIBOLA** WERE "ALL UNDER ONE LORD, THAT THE HOUSES, CONSTRUCTED OF STONE AND LIME WERE LARGE... THAT THE DOORWAYS OF THE PRINCIPAL HOUSES WERE MUCH ORNAMENTED WITH TURQUOISES, OF WHICH THERE WAS A GREAT ABUNDANCE, AND THAT THE PEOPLE OF THESE CITIES WENT VERY WELL CLOTHED."

YET ANOTHER MYTH IN LATINO HISTORY!

GASPAR PÉREZ DE VILLAGRÁ

WAS BORN IN PUEBLA, NEW SPAIN AROUND 1555. HE GRADUATED FROM THE UNIVERSITY OF SALAMANCA. WE KNOW HE WAS IN THE NEW WORLD AT THE AGE OF 25. PÉREZ DE VILLAGRÁ ACCOMPANIED JUAN DE OÑATE ON AN EXPEDITION TO CONQUER AND COLONIZE NEW MEXICO. HE WROTE THE EPIC POEM HISTORY OF NEW MEXICO IN 1610.

THERE ARE THINGS HIDDEN THAT ARE NOT CLEAR TO ME, LORD, FOR I HAVE ALWAYS BEEN AND AM A SAD AND DESPISED TRIFLING WORM.

THIS WAS, IN FACT, THE FIRST EPIC POEM TO BE COMPOSED IN NEW SPAIN. IT CHRONICLES OÑATE'S EXPEDITION AND DESCRIBES IN DETAIL THE BATTLES BETWEEN SPANISH KNIGHTS AND INDIANS. ACTUALLY, THE POEM'S LAST SEGMENT IS DEDICATED TO THE BATTLE OF EL PEÑOL DE ACOMA, WHERE MANY NATIVES DIED.

LET'S GO NEW MEXICO 1610

LET'S BE FRANK... HE WASN'T A VERY GOOD POET.

AT TIMES NEW SPAIN WAS ALSO CALLED NEW MEXICO. WHAT IS TODAY **NEW MEXICO** ALSO USED TO BE PART OF MEXICO.

TRUE, BUT VILLAGRÁ WAS COURAGEOUS. HIS IMAGES ARE MEMORABLE. PLUS, HE WAS THE FIRST..

NOT SO GOOD POET BY GASPAR DE L...

AND IN HISTORY, TO BE THE FIRST IS A TRIUMPH OF SORTS. WHO WAS THE FIRST TO CUT HIS NAILS WITH A NAIL TRIMMER?

SNIP
SNIP

PÉREZ DE VILLAGRÁ WROTE HIS POEM WHEN MIGUEL DE CERVANTES WAS ALREADY ENJOYING THE FRUITS OF THE FIRST PART OF DON QUIXOTE DE LA MANCHA AND WAS BEGINNING TO THINK UP A SECOND PART.

PÉREZ DE VILLAGRÁ EVENTUALLY RETURNED TO SPAIN. HE WAS ARRESTED AND FOUND GUILTY OF CRIMES COMMITTED DURING THE OÑATE EXPEDITION. (HE HAD EXECUTED TWO DESERTERS.) HIS PUNISHMENT: HE WAS BANISHED FROM NEW SPAIN FOR SIX YEARS. ALTHOUGH HE WAS LATER ALLOWED TO RETURN TO NEW SPAIN, HE DIED WHILE EN ROUTE TO GUATEMALA.

IS THE NEW WORLD REALLY "NEW"?

THE EXPANSE OF LAND STRETCHING FROM SOUTHEAST TEXAS TO SOUTHERN CALIFORNIA ATTRACTED MANY EXPLORERS LOOKING FOR FORTUNE. HOWEVER, THESE TERRITORIES — INCLUDING NEW MEXICO, ARIZONA AND PARTS OF COLORADO, UTAH AND NEVADA — WERE POPULATED BY SCATTERED INDIAN TRIBES OFTEN AT WAR WITH ONE ANOTHER. LOS ESPAÑOLES MIXED WITH THE NATIVES, CREATING A WHOLE NEW RACE, ESPECIALLY IN MEXICO: <u>LA RAZA MESTIZA</u>, THE MIXED RACE! OTHER EUROPEAN COLONISTS DID NOT INTRUDE IN THE LIFE OF THE INDIANS UNTIL THE SPANISH COLONIZERS DECIDED THE LAND WAS THEIR PROPERTY.

TO COLONIZE IS TO SUBDUE, TO RENAME, TO REDEFINE...

IT WASN'T ONLY THE INDIAN LAND THAT WAS THEIRS, BUT ALSO THE INDIAN BODY. THE COLONIZERS SHOWED THE NATIVES HOW TO DRESS AND EAT AS THEY DID. THEY TOOK ADVANTAGE OF THE INDIAN WOMEN AND IN MANY CASES, EVEN RAPED THEM. IN SHORT, THEY TRIED TO INSTILL MACHISMO AS A WAY OF LIFE FOR THE INDIANS.

ISN'T THAT A LINE BY ROBERT FROST — "THE LAND WAS OURS BEFORE WE WERE THE LAND'S"?

YES, BUT THE QUESTION IS: WHO IS "WE"? FOR CENTURIES THE INDIANS WERE NOT CONSIDERED A "WE", BUT A "THEY".

WHAT IF HISTORY WAS THE OTHER WAY AROUND? WHAT IF PRE-COLUMBIAN CIVILIZATION HAD ARRIVED IN EUROPE IN 1492, AND FORCED ITS RELIGIOUS BELIEFS AND WAY OF LIFE ON ITS EUROPEAN CITIZENS?

IL VATICANO

WE WOULDN'T HAVE A POPE, OR THE COUNTLESS CHURCHES AND PALACES ON BOTH SIDES OF THE ATLANTIC. MARTIN LUTHER WOULDN'T HAVE REBELLED AGAINST THE CATHOLIC CHURCH, SO PROTESTANTISM WOULDN'T EXIST.

THE WORLD WOULD BE A <u>VERY</u> DIFFERENT PLACE.'

THE SPANISH EMPIRE HAD TROUBLE "CIVILIZING" THE INDIANS. IN ADDITION TO PUSHING MACHISMO, THE COLONIZERS ALSO TRIED TO INDOCTRINATE THE INDIANS INTO THE CATHOLIC FAITH.

AND WHAT IF IT WERE THE SPANIARDS WHO WERE THE ONES BROUGHT BACK IN CAGES TO THE NEW WORLD?

WHAT IF OUR VIEW OF BEAUTY HAD INDIAN WOMEN - BRONZE, SVELTE, STUNNING - AS ITS IDEAL, AND NOT ITS IBERIAN COUNTERPARTS?

THE WINNER SETS THE RULES, NO?

LET'S NOT GET LOST IN NEEDLESS "IFS". OUR JOB IS TO CHRONICLE **LATINO HISTORY.**

THAT'S RIGHT! HE'S SO DISTRACTING!

As African slaves arrived in the West Indies, Brazil, Cuba, Mexico, and the U.S., other racial types emerged, such as mulattos and SAMBOS.

A mulatto is a person of mixed African and Caucasian heritage. A Sambo - also spelled Zambo - was the term used for an African person born in the Americas.

The racial mixture created a hierarchy based on whiteness - the whiter your skin color, the more respect you commanded.

HERNANDO de SOTO EXPLORES AREAS BETWEEN FLORIDA AND LOUISIANA.

TOURIST INFO

1538

1565

MACHO, MACHO MAN...

SPANISH KNIGHTS BEGIN BUILDING CHURCHES IN ST. AUGUSTINE, FLORIDA.

1565

FUTURE SITE OF TACO BELL

JUAN DE OÑATE BEGINS ESTABLISHING SPANISH TOWNS IN NORTHERN NEW MEXICO.

SANTA FÉ

THE OLDEST STATE CAPITAL IN THE SOUTHWEST IS **SANTA-FÉ**, FOUNDED IN **1610**. NEW MEXICO WAS THE TERRITORY THAT QUICKLY BEGAN TO COMMAND ATTENTION. THERE, SPANISH ECCLESIASTICAL AND POLITICAL POWER - THE "TWO MAJESTIES" - RULED SIMULTANEOUSLY. THESE TWO SIDES ENJOYED ATTACKING EACH OTHER. THE GOVERNORS ACCUSED

THE PRIESTS OF PERSONALLY BEN-EFITTING FROM THE INDIAN LABOR, AND THE PRIESTS COUNTERATTACKED BY ACCUSING THE POLITICIANS OF FOSTERING PAGANISM. IN 1645, THE COLONY WAS IN A STATE OF VIRTUAL CIVIL WAR. IN 1680, PUEBLO INDIANS REVOLTED.

THE REVOLT WAS LED BY **POPÉ** WHOM THE SPANIARDS CALLED A "WHIRLWIND." THE REVOLT WAS PLAN-NED FOR TWELVE YEARS, AND DROVE THE SPANIARDS TO EL PASO. THE INDIANS ALSO BURNED SANTA FÉ, AND WERE SUPPORTED BY MESTIZOS. TWELVE YEARS LATER THE SPAN-IARDS RETURNED WITH HEAVY WEA-PONRY AND MASSACRED A GREAT PORTION OF THE POPULATION.

SPAIN ESTABLISHED **MISIONES** TO HELP COLONIZE THE COAST OF CALIFORNIA AND PARTS OF TEXAS IN THESE MISIONES. INDIANS AND MESTIZOS WERE INDOCTRINATED INTO THE CHRISTIAN FAITH. BRUTAL BEATINGS AND OVERWORK RESULTED IN COUNTLESS CASES OF DISEASE AND THE DEATH OF THREE MILLION PEOPLE BETWEEN THE END OF THE SEVENTENTH AND THE END OF THE EIGHTEENTH CENTURY.

BUT NOT ALL WAS CRUELTY AND DESTRUCTION. PROGRESS WAS ALSO ACHIEVED ALBEIT SLOWLY, AMONG THE CHRISTIAN MISSIONAR-IES.

IT IS OF THE UTMOST IMPORTANCE THAT THE **MISIONES** BE PROVIDED WITH LABORERS, TO FILL THE LAND, AND SO RAISE THE CROPS OF THEIR MAINTENANCE AND PROGRESS... WE ARE POOR AND NEED ALL THE HELP WE CAN GET FROM YOUR EXCELLENCY, THE KING...

REPORT ON THE GENERAL CONDITIONS AND NEEDS OF THE MISSIONS OF UPPER CALIFORNIA

INDIO BURIALS 9AM

FATHER JUNÍPERO SERRA,

A FRANCISCAN MISSIONARY, WAS BORN IN 1713 IN MALLORCA AND DIED IN 1784. HE DID MISSIONS WORK IN CALIFORNIA, HELPING TO ESTABLISH MISIONES ACROSS THE REGION AND FIGHTING FOR THEIR CONTINUANCE DESPITE HIS MANY PHYSICAL AILMENTS. HE WAS INSTRUMENTAL IN THE ESTABLISHMENT OF OF 21 FRANCISCAN MISIONES BETWEEN 1769 AND 1823, FROM SAN DIEGO TO MONTEREY. HE ALSO ORCHESTRATED THE EXPEDITION OF JUAN BAUTISTA DE ANZA THAT FOUNDED THE CITY OF SAN FRANCISCO.

HIS FACE WAS ON A U.S. STAMP, AND MANY STATUES WERE ERECTED IN HIS HONOR.

A STATE PARK IN CALIFORNIA IS ALSO NAMED AFTER HIM.

24

The American revolution accentuated the need for Mexico to secede from Spain and Portugal. The ideas of **ENLIGHTENMENT** and revolution, the goals of equality, progress, and free enterprise swept the southern hemisphere following the French revolution in 1789.

Books: Founding Father Natural Born Killers / The Jeffersons Tom Andreezy Indian Killing For Dummies / All Men Are Created Equal Except You / Pocho Masato Anthology

AY TÚ, AUTOR!

WOULD MEXICO BECOME MODERN? HOW DOES ONE BECOME MODERN? MODERNITY IS A STATE OF MIND?

¡MEXICANOS, LA LIBERTAD ES NUESTRA!

¡ABAJO CON ESPAÑA!

MIGUEL HIDALGO Y COSTILLA

JOSÉ MARÍA MORELOS Y PAVÓN

THE WAR OF INDEPENDENCE IN MEXICO TOOK PLACE IN 1810. IT WAS LED BY CATHOLIC CRIOLLO PRIESTS SEEKING TO MODEL THE COUNTRY AFTER FRANCE AND THE UNITED STATES. BUT WHEN MEXICO FOUND ITSELF AN INDEPENDENT NATION IN 1821, IT ALSO REALIZED HOW POOR, AWKWARD AND EXHAUSTED A NATION IT WAS.

VACANT

THE EXPANSIVE DREAM OF THE UNITED STATES HAD A NAME. IT WAS CALLED **"THE DOCTRINE OF MANIFEST DESTINY."**

THE BORDERS OF THE UNITED STATES GREW CONSIDERABLY IN THE NINETEENTH CENTURY. FIRST WAS THE LOUISIANA PURCHASE IN 1803, WHEN THE UNITED STATES BOUGHT LOUISIANA FROM NAPOLEON BONAPARTE. IN 1819, FLORIDA WAS TAKEN BY FORCE FROM SPAIN. ENGLAND LOST OREGON TO THE UNITED STATES IN 1846.

HE COULD SKIP A MEAL!

FLORIDA
LOUISIANA PURCHASE
CALIFORNIA
TEXAS
NEW MEXICO
COLORADO
ARIZONA

MANIFEST DESTINY

ANGLO-SAXONS WERE SLOW IN COMING TO THE SOUTHWEST, BUT GRADUALLY TOOK HOLD, PARTICULARLY IN TEXAS. THE SPANISH AND MEXICAN GOVERNMENTS ENCOURAGED THIS TYPE OF "FOREIGN IMMIGRATION" BUT SOON THE MEXICAN GOVERNMENT WAS ALARMED AND IN THE FAMOUS "DECREE OF APRIL 6, 1830," IT PROHIBITED ANY FURTHER IMMIGRATION FROM THE U.S.

PRESIDENT ANDREW JACKSON, ALONG WITH HIS FRIEND SAM HOUSTON, SOUGHT WAYS TO INCORPORATE TEXAS INTO THE UNION.

28

AH, REMEMBER THE ALAMO! BUT, ¿QUIÉN SE ACUERDA DEL ALAMO?

HISTORY BOOKS TELL US ONLY HALF THE STORY ABOUT THE FAMOUS 12 DAY **BATTLE OF THE ALAMO** IN **1836.** ENGLISH-SPEAKING TEXTS GLORIFY THE AMERICANS, EVEN THOUGH THEY LOST, AND CELEBRATE SAM HOUSTON AS THE FIRST PRESIDENT OF THE "REPUBLIC OF TEXAS." THE MEXICANS ARE CONDEMNED AS TRAITORS AND RUFFIANS.

BUT THE STORY IS MORE COMPLEX! FOR INSTANCE, MEXICO HAD RECENTLY ANNOUNCED IT WOULD FREE ALL SLAVES IN TEXAS, WHICH SHOCKED THE ANGLO-SAXONS. TEXAS HAD MANY GRIEVANCES AGAINST MEXICO.

JAMES BOWIE   WILLIAM TRAVIS   DAVEY CROCKETT

IT IS IMPORTANT TO UNDERSTAND THAT HISTORY BOOKS DON'T ALWAYS TELL THE WHOLE STORY! MOST ANGLO TEXTS OVERLOOK THE RICHNESS OF MEXICAN CULTURE.
ON THE OTHER HAND, THEY FAIL TO MENTION THE DUBIOUS PASTS OF THE AMERICAN LEADERS. JAMES BOWIE WAS A SLAVE TRADER WHO MADE A FORTUNE SELLING SLAVES IN LOUISIANA.
DAVEY CROCKETT HAD KILLED INDIANS IN FLORIDA. WILLIAM TRAVIS COMMITTED A CRIME IN ALABAMA BUT ALLOWED A SLAVE TO BE CONDEMNED TO DEATH FOR IT.

THE MEXICAN ARMY, WITH MORE THAN 6,000 MEN, SHOWED UP IN SAN ANTONIO ON FEBRUARY 23, 1863, AND LAID SIEGE TO THE ALAMO, A MISSION THAT HAD BEEN CONVERTED INTO A FORTRESS. ONLY 187 TEXANS DEFENDED THE PLACE. ON MARCH 6, THE MEXICANS ASSAULTED THE FORTRESS, CAPTURING IT, AND KILLING THE DEFENDERS. THE ONLY SURVIVOR - SO THE LEGEND GOES - WAS A SERVANT WHO CRIED "REMEMBER THE ALAMO"!

NO ONE WAS TRULY VICTORIOUS. MEXICO MIGHT HAVE WON THE BATTLE, BUT MANY MEXICANS WERE KILLED. AND THE TEXANS SUFFERED A TERRIBLE DEFEAT.

THE TEXAS REVOLUTION OF 1835-36 HAD MUCH TO DO WITH MEXICO'S DICTATOR **ANTONIO LÓPEZ DE SANTA ANNA.**

YOU'RE WELCOME!

HE HAD CANCELED THE CONSTITUTION OF 1824 AND DECLARED HIMSELF SOLE RULER OF THE NATION. TEXAS WAS READY TO ESTABLISH ITS INDEPENDENCE. THE FIRST BATTLE WAS WON BY THE TEXANS IN SAN ANTONIO. THE DEFEAT OF MEXICAN MILITARY LEADER GENERAL MARTÍN PERFECTO de COS BECAME A SOURCE OF ENORMOUS SHAME TO SANTA ANNA. BUT THE SECOND BATTLE, THE ALAMO, WAS A MEXICAN VICTORY. FIVE DAYS BEFORE, TEXAS HAD DECLARED ITS INDEPENDENCE FROM MEXICO.

SANTA ANNA, THE VILLAIN. WOULD ANYBODY IN THE U.S. TODAY RECOGNIZE SANTA ANNA IF IT WASN'T FOR THE HOLLYWOOD MOVIE **THE ALAMO**, WITH JOHN WAYNE? IT WAS RELEASED IN 1960, AND RUBEN PADILLA PLAYED GENERALÍSIMO SANTA ANA.

THERE HAVE BEEN FOUR MOVIES ABOUT THE ALAMO. COMPARED TO THE OTHERS, JOHN WAYNE'S IS A MASTER-PIECE OF ARTISTIC ACCOMPLISHMENT AND MORAL BALANCE. BUT I STILL DOUBT THAT WITH OR WITHOUT JOHN WAYNE, PEOPLE WOULD KNOW WHO SANTA ANNA WAS...

REMEMBER THE ALAMO, the movie

IN APRIL THE ARMY OF **SAM HOUSTON** DEFEATED SANTA ANNA.

TEXAS DID NOT BECOME PART OF THE UNION UNTIL 1844, AFTER THE ELECTION OF PRESIDENT JAMES POLK.

BUT POLK ALSO WANTED TO BUY OTHER TERRITORIES FROM MEXICO— CALIFORNIA AND NEW MEXICO AMONG THEM.

SANTA ANNA WAS AGAINST SUCH EXPANSION

I DECLARE MY PURPOSE TO ACQUIRE CALIFORNIA AND NEW MEXICO FOR THE UNITED STATES, AND PERHAPS OTHER NORTHERN PROVINCES OF MEXICO.

POLK

THE WHOLE AFFAIR ENDED IN THE SO-CALLED MEXICAN-AMERICAN WAR. ITS ROOTS WERE IN THE EXPANSIONIST POLICIES OF THE WHITE HOUSE. ALSO, AN ECONOMIC DEPRESSION HAD SWEPT THE U.S. IN 1837. THE DEPRESSION IN THE NORTHEAST MADE IT NECESSARY TO LOOK FOR NEW MARKETS TO ACCOMMODATE THE EVER-INCREASING MERCHANDISE.

THE WAR BROKE OUT IN 1846. PRESIDENT POLK SENT TROOPS NEAR MATAMOROS, MEXICO. THE MEXICAN ARMY FOUGHT BACK, AND THE U.S. ACCUSED IT OF "INVADING AMERICAN TERRITORY." SO THE U.S. MILITARY ATTACKED THE CITY OF MONTERREY, MEXICO (THE CAPITAL OF THE STATE OF NUEVO LEÓN) AND MARCHED INTO SANTA FÉ AND TAOS.

Mexican Treacheries and Cruelties

INCIDENTS AND SUFFERINGS

IN THE

MEXICAN WAR;

Also, an Account of Valiant Soldiers Fallen

18 — 47

THE WAR WAS FOUGHT ON MANY FRONTS, MOST IMPORTANTLY IN THE MEDIA.

IN FACT, HISTORIANS BELIEVE THE MEXICAN-AMERICAN WAR IS THE FIRST TO HAVE USED MEDIA TACTICS TO GENERATE PUBLIC SUPPORT.

MEXICANS WERE PORTRAYED AS LAZY DRUNKARDS AND GOOD-FOR-NOTHINGS.

THE MEXICAN REPORT

-HIC-
DOH
-HIC-

PRESIDENT POLK COMMANDED GENERAL WINFIELD SCOTT TO GO ALL THE WAY TO THE HEART OF THE ENEMY. THE U.S. ARMY FIRST INVADED THE GULF PORT OF VERACRUZ, SETTING THE WHOLE CITY IN FLAMES. MANY CIVILIANS DIED.

MEXICAN PEASANTS AND URBAN DWELLERS DIDN'T QUITE KNOW HOW TO GREET THE GRINGOS. THE MEXICAN ARMY FOUGHT, OF COURSE, BUT COMMON MEN AND WOMEN WERE FRIENDLY.

I CAN SCARCELY BELIEVE THAT WE ARE IN AN ENEMY COUNTRY. THE MEXICANS PASS MY TENT EVERY MINUTE WITH SUGAR, BREAD, CHEESE, ORANGES, POTATOES, ONIONS AND SO ON, FOR SALE.

HOT FÚD FOR SALE

ON **MAY 15, 1847,** GENERAL SCOTT AND HIS TROOPS ENTERED PUEBLA DE LOS ANGELES, MEXICO'S SECOND LARGEST CITY. THEY REMAINED THERE FOR A SUMMER, WAITING FOR REINFORCEMENTS TO RENEW THE CAMPAIGN.

IN SPITE OF THE MEXICAN'S GOODWILL, NEWSPAPERS IN THE U.S. DESCRIBED THE PUEBLANS AS "SOMBER and UNFRIENDLY."

IRONY OF IRONIES: MORE THAN A CENTURY LATER, THOUSANDS OF PUEBLANS WOULD EMIGRATE TO NEW YORK AND ELSEWHERE IN NEW ENGLAND, REVITALIZING THE REGION'S ECONOMY AND BRINGING IN A JOYOUS SPIRIT.

"THE CITY OF PUEBLA CONTAINS ONE HUNDRED THOUSAND INHABITANTS, TEN THOUSAND OF WHOM AT LEAST WERE ABLE TO BEAR ARMS; AND THESE, BACKED AND SUPPORTED BY A HOSTILE POPULATION OF EIGHTY THOUSAND, WERE STANDING QUIETLY BY, AND LOOKING ON WHEN THE GATES OF THE CITY WERE OPENED, AND AN ARMY OF FOUR THOUSAND TWO HUNDRED MEN ENTERED THE ANGEL TROD STREETS OF THIS CELESTIAL CITY, AND TOOK PEACEABLE POSSESSION OF IT WITHOUT FIRING A GUN. MANY OF THE CITIZENS AND FOREIGN RESIDENTS, IN SPEAKING AFTERWARDS OF OUR ENTRY INTO THE CITY, ACKNOWLEDGED THEMSELVES PERFECTLY ASTONISHED AT THE COOL AND CARELESS INDIFFERENCE THAT SEEMED TO CHARACTERIZE EVERY MOVEMENT OF THE AMERICAN ARMY WHILE SUCH IMMINENT DANGER ENCOMPASSED THEM ON ALL SIDES."

WHOM TO BELIEVE, EXCEPT MY MOTHER, OF COURSE?

EVENTUALLY, SCOTT AND HIS ARMY ARRIVED IN CIUDAD DE MÉXICO.

A TRAGIC DAY!

IN THE FAMOUS BATTLE OF SEPTEMBER 12-13, 1847, THE U.S. ARMY FOUGHT THE MEXICANS AT THE CASTLE OF CHAPULTEPEC. THE FIGHT LASTED FOURTEEN HOURS. IN THE END, MEXICO SURRENDERED BUT NOT BEFORE A FEARLESS ACT WAS PERFORMED. SIX YOUNG CADETS, KNOWN IN MEXICO AS **LOS NIÑOS HÉROES**, REALIZING THAT DEFEAT WAS UNAVOIDABLE, REACHED THE ROOF OF THE CASTLE, COVERED THEMSELVES WITH THE MEXICAN FLAG AND JUMPED TO THEIR DEATHS.

JUAN ESCUTIA

FERNANDO MONTES DE OCA

FRANCISCO MÁRQUEZ

AGUSTÍN MELGAR

VICENTE SUAREZ

JUAN DE LA BARRERA

BUT DID THE EVENT REALLY HAPPEN? IS IT ONLY A USEFUL MYTH DEVISED BY A DEFEATED NATION TO RAISE ITS MORALE? A GROUP OF AMERICAN HISTORIANS PROVED, IN THE LATE 1970's, THAT NONE OF THE NAMES APPEAR IN THE REGISTRATION ARCHIVES OF THE ESCUELA MILITAR THAT WAS HOUSED AT THE CASTLE OF CHAPULTEPEC AT THE TIME. A CONVENIENT LIE?

WHAT IS HISTORY IF NOT A SET OF CONVENIENT COLLECTIBLE LIES - A FICTION?

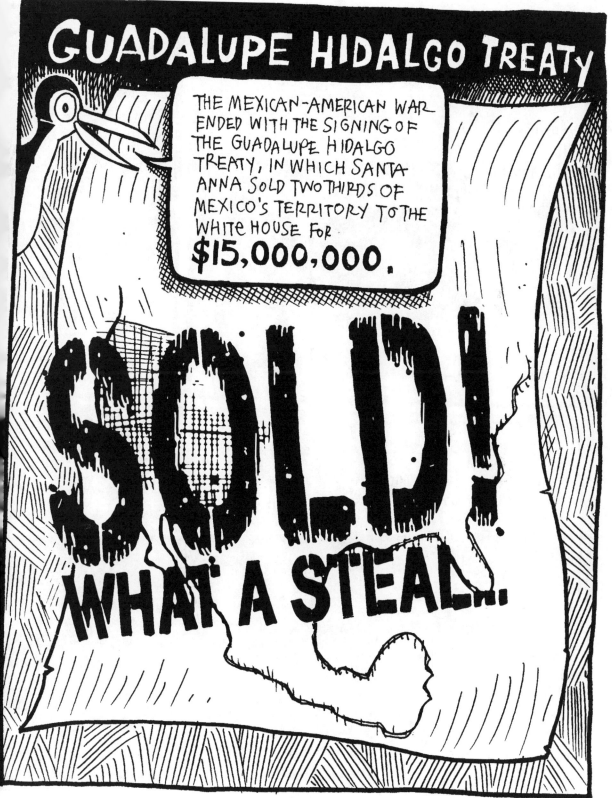

IN MEXICO, A FAMOUSLY CRUEL JOKE CLAIMS THAT THE COUNTRY HAD BEEN IN SUCH A TERRIBLE STATE BECAUSE OF TWO MAJOR HISTORICAL MISTAKES. FIRST, HERNÁN CORTÉS DIDN'T FULLY DESTROY THE AZTEC EMPIRE, HE ONLY SUBDUED IT. HAD HE REALLY "DESTROYED" IT, HISTORY WOULD HAVE BEEN TOTALLY DIFFERENT.

AND SECOND?

THE SECOND MISTAKE WAS SANTA ANNA'S. HE ONLY SOLD TWO-THIRDS OF THE MEXICAN TERRITORY, NOT THE WHOLE THING.

¡!

SOME HISTORIANS ARGUE THAT LATINO HISTORY PER SE REALLY BEGINS AT THIS POINT, WHEN A CONSIDERABLE NUMBER OF MEXICANS SUDDENLY FOUND THEMSELVES LIVING WITHIN THE GEOGRAPHICAL BOUNDARIES OF THE UNITED STATES.

TREATY

¡!

IN THE NAME OF ALMIGHTY GOD:

THE UNITED STATES OF AMERICA, AND THE UNITED MEXICAN STATES, ANIMATED BY A SINCERE DESIRE TO PUT AN END TO THE CALAMITIES OF THE WAR WHICH UNHAPPILY EXISTS BETWEEN THE TWO REPUBLICS, AND TO ESTABLISH UPON A SOLID BASIS RELATIONS OF PEACE AND FRIENDSHIP, WHICH SHALL CONFER RECIPROCAL BENEFITS UPON THE CITIZENS OF BOTH, AND ASSURE THE CONCORD, HARMONY AND MUTUAL CONFIDENCE WHEREIN THE TWO PEOPLE SHOULD LIVE. AS GOOD NEIGHBORS ... [HAVE SIGNED THIS] TREATY OF PEACE, FRIENDSHIPS, LIMITS AND SETTLEMENTS ...

Article VIII

Mexicans now established in territories previously belonging to Mexico, and which remain for the future within the limits of the United States, as defined by the present treaty, shall be free to continue where they now reside, or to return at any time to the Mexican Republic, retaining the property which they posses in the said territiories, or disposing thereof, and removing the proceeds wherever they please; without their being subjected, on this account, to any contribution, tax or change whatever.

Article IX

The Mexicans who, in the territories aforementioned, shall not preserve the character of citizens of the Mexican republic, comfortably with what is stipulated in the preceding article, shall be incorporated into the Union of the United States and be admitted, at the proper time (to be judged of by the Congress of the United States) to the enjoyment of all the rights of citizens...

THIS MEANS MEXICANS COULD DECIDE TO BECOME U.S. CITIZENS OR PACK THEIR BAGS AND LEAVE FOR MEXICO. A DIFFICULT CHOICE, DON'T YOU THINK? WHAT WOULD YOU DO? REMAIN IN ENEMY LAND?

IT WASN'T THAT SIMPLE! MOST MEXICAN FRONTIER DWELLERS IN NEW MEXICO, CALIFORNIA, AND ARIZONA HAD AMBIVALENT FEELINGS TOWARD THE CORRUPT GOVERNMENT IN CIUDAD DE MEXICO, AND ESPECIALLY TOWARD SANTA ANNA.

AND WHAT ABOUT THE SPANISH LANGUAGE? WAS IT DECLARED ILLEGAL? WAS THE ENGLISH LANGUAGE FORCED ON THOSE IN THE NEWLY ACQUIRED TERRITORIES?

THE ISSUE OF LANGUAGE WAS COMPLICATED. ENGLISH WAS QUICKLY INSTALLED AS THE BUSINESS TONGUE, FORCING SPANISH INTO THE PRIVATE DOMESTIC REALM.

‹ESPAÑOL›

IN MEXICO, THE ANNEXATION OF THE SOUTHWEST WAS SEEN AS A THREAT. PRESIDENT JOSÉ J. HERRERA BELIEVED IT WAS A PLOY BY THE U.S. TO FURTHER EXPAND INTO MEXICAN TERRITORY. JOSE M. ROA BÁRCENA BELIEVED IT WAS THE RESULT OF MEXICO'S SHORTSIGHTED FOREIGN POLICY. JORGE L. TAMAYO, IN HIS 1848 BOOK LO QUE PERDIMOS Y LO QUE NOS QUEDA, CALLED ATTENTION TO THE MEXICAN GOVERNMENT'S NEGLECT OF ITS NORTHERN FRONTIERS. IGNACIO MANUEL ALTAMIRANO SUGGESTED THE DEFEAT WAS THE RESULT OF INEPT GENERALS AND COLONELS IN THE MEXICAN ARMY.

IN THE 1960's, HISTORIAN DANIEL COSÍO VILLEGAS PROVIDED A LARGER VIEW

1964

"SO MEXICO AND THE UNITED STATES ARE DIFFERENT COUNTRIES. AND THEIR PATHS DIFFER ALSO. NEVERTHELESS, THEY HAVE NOT BEEN ABLE TO GO THEIR DIFFERENT WAYS; THEY ARE NEIGHBORS, WHETHER THEIR INTERESTS COINCIDE OR CLASH... [THE ANNEXATION OF TEXAS] WAS THE FIRST ADJUSTMENT MEXICO HAD TO MAKE IN THE CRUSHING PROCESS TO WHICH IT HAS BEEN SUBJECTED, TO WHICH IT IS STILL SUBJECTED BECAUSE OF ITS GOOD NEIGHBORHOOD WITH THE U.S.

IN THE SECOND HALF OF THE NINETEENTH CENTURY, THE SOUTHWEST MOVED TOWARD INDUSTRIALIZATION. RAILROADS WERE BUILT ALL ACROSS THE REGION, GOLD MINES BECAME PROFITABLE, AND AMERICANIZED **RANCHEROS** COULD BE FOUND EVERYWHERE FROM TEXAS TO UTAH.

ALL THIS, OF COURSE, RESULTED IN DRAMATIC SETBACKS FOR THE MEXICAN POPULATION. THE "RESPECT" ENDORSED BY THE TREATY OF GUADALUPE HIDALGO WAS PURE FICTION

MEXICANS WERE FORCED ECONOMICALLY AND SOMETIMES PHYSICALLY TO PERFORM MENIAL JOBS AND TO WORK THE GOLD MINES. THE TENSION BETWEEN ANGLOS & MEXICANS WAS UNAVOIDABLE.

ON THE OTHER HAND, WITH THE ARRIVAL OF ANGLO CULTURE, MONEY CAME THROUGH.

JUAN CORTINA

GREGORIO CORTEZ

TIBURCIO VÁZQUEZ

JOAQUIN MURRIETA

A NUMBER OF FOLK HEROES EMERGED ON THE U.S.-MEXICO BORDER WHO CAME TO SYMBOLIZE THE MEXICAN RESISTANCE TO ANGLO OPPRESSION.

MANY OF THESE HEROES BEHAVED LIKE ROBIN HOOD: THEY STOLE FROM THE RICH AND GAVE TO THE POOR. THEIR ROOTS WERE MEXICAN AND THEIR COURAGE MADE THEM LEGENDARY. THEY ARE THE ORIGINAL BANDIDOS - OUTLAWS.

GREGORIO CORTEZ WAS A BELOVED FIGURE AMONG THE HAVE-NOTS IN 1900 TEXAS.

39

THE PLIGHT OF GREGORIO CORTEZ

GREGORIO CORTEZ WAS IN HIS HOME IN EL CARMEN, TEXAS, SHAVING NEAR HIS FAMILY.

A SHERIFF COMES TO ASK HIM ABOUT A MISSING MARE. CORTEZ MIS-UNDERSTANDS HIM.

THE SHERIFF SHOOTS CORTEZ'S BROTHER.

CORTEZ SHOOTS THE SHERIFF, THUS BECOMING AN OUTLAW.

REWARD $3,000 DEAD OR ALIVE

THE AUTHORITIES ANNOUNCE A REWARD OF $3,000 TO CAPTURE CORTEZ AND HE IS SOUGHT BY SHERIFFS + RANGERS.

CORTEZ ELUDES THE AUTHORITIES

BUT EVENTUALLY HE IS CAPTURED.

AND HE'S PUT ON TRIAL. CORTEZ IS FOUND NOT GUILTY, BUT ONE OF HIS ENEMIES FINDS A SOLUTION:

TO ONCE AGAIN PUT HIM ON TRIAL FOR HAVING STOLEN A MARE. HE'S FOUND GUILTY AND SENTENCED TO 99 YEARS AND A DAY.

LESS THAN A YEAR LATER, ABRAHAM LINCOLN'S DAUGHTER ASKS THE TEXAS GOVERNOR FOR CLEMENCY.

CORTEZ IS SET FREE! BUT HIS ENEMIES END UP POISONING HIM. HE'S BURIED SOMEWHERE IN MATAMOROS, BROWNSVILLE OR LAREDO.

G. CORTEZ

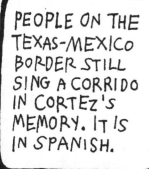

PEOPLE ON THE TEXAS-MEXICO BORDER STILL SING A CORRIDO IN CORTEZ'S MEMORY. IT IS IN SPANISH.

A CORRIDO IS A BORDER SONG - A **BALLAD** - CELEBRATING THE LIFE AND ACHIEVEMENTS OF A FOLK HERO.

THIS IS HOW PARTS OF IT WOULD GO IN ENGLISH. ITS BEAUTY IS LOST IN THE TRANSLATION.

YO NO SOY AMERICANO
PERO COMPRENDO EL INGLÉS
YO LO APRENDÍ CON MI HERMANO
AL DERECHO Y AL REVÉS
A CUALQUIER AMERICANO
LO HAGO
TEMBLAR A MIS PIES

"The Ballad of Gregorio Cortez"

In the county of El Carmen
Look what has happened;
The Major Sheriff died,
Leaving Román badly wounded.

The next day, in the morning,
When people arrived,
They said to one another,
"It is known who killed him."

They went around asking questions,
About three hours afterward;
They found the wrongdoer
Has been Gregorio Cortez.

Now they have outlawed Cortez
Throughout the whole state;
Let him be taken, dead or alive;
He has killed several men.

Then said Gregorio Cortez,
with his pistol in his hand,
"I don't regret that I killed him;
I regret my brother's death."

The Americans were coming;
They seemed to fly through the air;
Because they were going to get
Three thousand dollars they offered.

He struck out for Gonzales;
Several sheriffs saw him;
They decided not to follow
Because they were
afraid of him.

GREGORIO CORTEZ
T-SHIRTS XL ONLY

POOR GREGORIO CORTEZ, NEVER MADE IT INTO THE AMERICAN IMAGINATION...

HOW ABOUT "LA CUCARACHA?"

THE METAMORPHOSIS Francisco Kafka

LA CUCARACHA, LA CUCARACHA
RUNNING UP AND DOWN THE HOUSE
LA CUCARACHA LA CUCARACHA
QUIET AS A LITTLE MOUSE
HE GETS IN TROUBLE A LOT OF TROUBLE
SNOOPING HERE AND EVERYWHERE
LA CUCARACHA LA CUCARACHA
ALWAYS KEEPS THE CUPBOARD BARE...

OR THE SPANISH VERSION:

LA CUCARACHA LA CUCARACHA
YA NO PUEDE CAMINAR
PORQUE NO TIENE, PORQUE LE FALTA
MARIGUANA QUE FUMAR

NOW IS THAT A FAMOUS CORRIDO OR WHAT? GRACIAS VERY MUCH.

JOAQUIN MURRIETA WAS A MEXICAN MINER WHO EMIGRATED TO CALIFORNIA AROUND 1850. DIFFERENT VERSIONS OF HIS LEGEND ARE CONTRADICTORY. SOME SAY HIS WIFE WAS RAPED, OTHERS THAT HE HIMSELF WAS BEATEN BY ANGLOS. MURRIETA FOUGHT BACK AND MANY PEOPLE SUPPORTED AND FOLLOWED HIM. IT IS SAID HE WAS KILLED BY THE TEXAS RANGERS AND HIS BODY DECAPITATED.

PABLO NERUDA, THE POET, DISSIDENT AND NOBEL PRIZE WINNER, WROTE A PLAY ABOUT MURRIETA, AND CLAIMED MURRIETA WAS ACTUALLY CHILEAN!

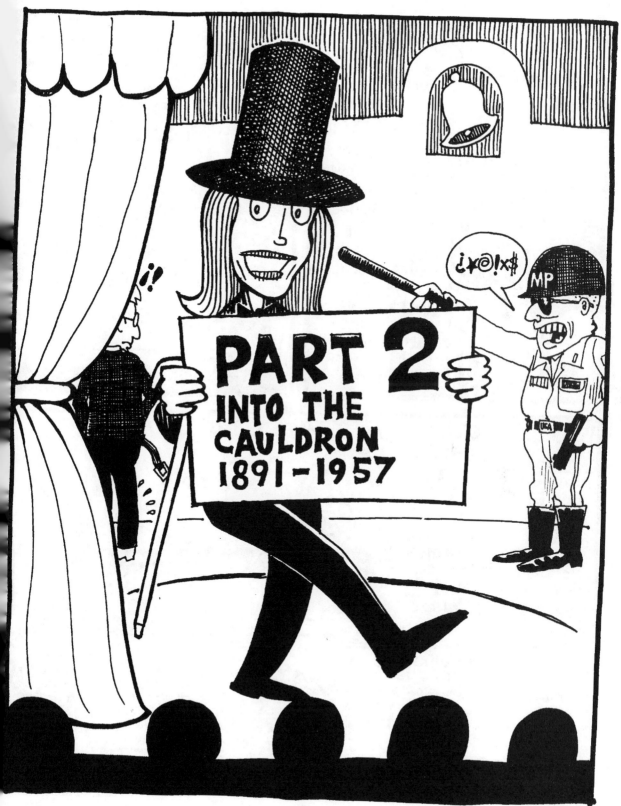

WHAT DID THE **GOOD NEIGHBOR POLICY** STAND FOR?

IN SPANISH IT WAS CALLED "LA POLITICA DEL BUEN VECINO." IT WAS IMPLEMENTED BY PRESIDENT FRANKLIN DELANO ROOSEVELT. IT WAS DEVISED SO THAT THE ALMIGHTY UNITED STATES WOULD ALLOW LATIN AMERICAN NATIONS TO CHOOSE THEIR OWN GOVERNMENT WITHOUT INTERFERENCE.

LESSON #1 — H

1935 FDR

BUT IT WAS SELDOM IMPLEMENTED.

IN FACT, IT ONLY SERVED TO STRESS THE DIVISION BETWEEN THE HAVES AND THE HAVE-NOTS, SAY BETWEEN FLORIDA AND SAN JUAN.

FDR

TODAY

WALT DISNEY CREATED *THE THREE CABALLEROS* IN THE LATE THIRTIES AFTER ROOSEVELT INVITED HIM TO VISIT SOUTH AMERICA AND PRODUCE AN ANIMATED MOTION PICTURE PORTRAYING THE NEIGHBORS SOUTH OF THE RIO GRANDE AS BENIGN SIMPÁTICOS.

THE RESULTS WERE DISASTROUS! THE MOVIE DEPICTED THE SPANISH-SPEAKING WORLD AS LUSTFUL, TREACHEROUS AND ON AN ETERNAL QUEST FOR LEISURE.

AH, THE RECURRENCE OF STEREOTYPES! SHALL I BUY A SOMBRERO AND A BOTTLE OF TEQUILA SAUZA? LET'S WATCH STEVE MARTIN'S "MAN WITH TWO BRAINS?"

HEY, TAKE A LOOK AT FLORIDA. IT'S ALSO PART OF THE CARIBBEAN BASIN. ITS TROPICAL SPIRIT IS SHARED WITH CUBA, PUERTO RICO, THE DOMINICAN, REPUBLIC, AND ELSEWHERE IN THE ANTILLES.

IN THE 1960's, PEOPLE BEGAN USING THE TERM "FIRST WORLD" AND "THIRD WORLD" TO DESCRIBE THE DIFFERENCE BETWEEN INDUSTRIALIZED, DEVELOPED NATIONS AND NATIONS WITH LESS DEVELOPED, MORE VULNERABLE ECONOMIES.

45

BUT THE DIFFERENCE WAS NOT ALWAYS THAT SHARP...

...AND PAINFUL.

THE **CARIBBEAN BASIN** WAS THE THEATER WHERE PIRATES SOUGHT THEIR FORTUNE.

AT LEAST NOT IN THE WHOLE CARIBBEAN REGION. **CUBA** FOR EXAMPLE WAS ALWAYS KNOWN AS "THE PEARL OF THE ANTILLES." IN COLONIAL TIMES, IT SERVED AS A PORT OF ARRIVAL AND DEPARTURE WHERE EUROPEAN GOODS EN ROUTE TO THE AMERICAS CHANGED SHIPS.

NOT ONLY PIRATES ABOUNDED IN THE CARIBBEAN. THE SLAVE TRADE WAS ALSO INTENSE. THOUSANDS OF SLAVES WERE SHIPPED FROM AFRICA TO NORTH AMERICAN AND LATIN AMERICAN SHORES. THEIR HARROWING EXPERIENCE AT SEA IS KNOWN AS **MIDDLE PASSAGE!**

-ye Cargoe-

THE AFRICANS ARRIVED IN AN ALIEN LAND, WITH AN ALIEN LANGUAGE AND AN ALIEN CIVILIZATION.

DIAGRAM OF THE SLAVE SHIP BROOKS.

SLAVE TRADE WAS JUSTIFIED DIFFERENTLY IN DIFFERENT PLACES IN VIRGINIA, THE TRADE WAS JUSTIFIED BY ARGUING THAT TOBACCO INDUSTRY PROFITS REQUIRED LOW COST LABOR.

IN MEXICO, THE CARIBBEAN REGION AND SOME PARTS OF NORTH-EASTERN SOUTH AMERICA, THE IBERIAN COLONIZERS HAD ALREADY FORCED THE INDIAN POPULATION INTO SLAVERY. IN THE FAMOUS **BLACK LEGEND** SPREAD BY FRAY BARTOLOME DE LAS CASAS AND OTHERS, SPANIARDS WERE ACCUSED OF NATIVE ABUSE.

BACK IN 1517...

AND SO FRAY BARTOLOMÉ DE LAS CASAS, KNOWN AS THE "APOSTLE OF THE INDIES," WHO RECOGNIZED THE CRUELTIES THE SPANISH SOLDIERS PERFORMED TO ACHIEVE THEIR GOALS OF COLONIZATION AND SPREAD THE SO-CALLED "BLACK LEGEND," THROUGH WHICH HE ACCUSED THE PERPETRATORS OF VIOLENCE, HAD AN EXTRAORDINARY IDEA: HE WOULD WRITE TO KING CHARLES V, EXPRESSING PITY FOR THE SUFFERING INDIANS AND RECOMMENDING THE IMPORT OF AFRICAN SLAVES

¡LA IMPORTACION DE LOS NEGROS! IN FRAY BARTOLOME'S MIND, AFRICANS WERE CLOSER TO MONKEYS ON THE NATURAL SCALE. THIS MEANT THEIR SUFFERING WAS PERCEIVED AS NOT QUITE HUMAN, AND THUS JUSTIFIABLE.

48

49

IN **1898**, THE **SPANISH AMERICAN WAR** WAS FOUGHT. THE WAR DID NOTHING BUT REPLACE THE SPANIARDS AS THE DOMINATING FORCE IN CUBA AND PUERTO RICO... WITH THE **UNITED STATES.**

BUT IT WAS MORE COMPLICATED, OBVIOUSLY. AFTER ALMOST FOUR LONG CENTURIES OF SPANISH DOMINATION IN CUBA IT WAS COLONIZED IN 1511—EDUCATED ELITE CUBANS PERCEIVED SPAIN AS THE UNWELCOME RULER. WITHIN THE ISLAND, THE SPIRIT OF INDEPENDENCE SPREAD.

(SPAIN'S SENSE OF JUSTICE) CG BUSH 1898

PIZARRO

CORTES

RIVA

THIS CARTOON FROM 1898 DEPICTS SPAIN'S PORTRAYAL BY THE U.S. AT THE TIME.

SPAIN

IN THE U.S.'S EYES, SPAIN AS A NATION, HAD ONE OF THE WORST RECORDS OF HUMAN ABUSE. HARPERS ACCUSED THE SPANISH HOLY OFFICE ...

THAT'S THE INQUISITION!

... OF SETTING LOOSE DOGS IN THE WEST INDIES TO TEAR INDIANS APART; THE DESTRUCTION OF THE AZTEC EMPIRE, THE KILLING OF INCA ATAHUALPA IN PERU, ETC. SPANIARDS WERE CONSIDERED SATAN INCARNATE

THAT'S CHARLES FRANCIS ADAMS, PRESIDENT OF THE UNIVERSITY OF WISCONSIN. AND THAT'S THE GRADUATING CLASS OF 1897. THE Q+A SYMBOLIZES A LONG-STANDING TRADITION OF STEREOTYPING.

WHAT GREAT BOOKS?

ZZZZ

WHAT HAS SPAIN EVER DONE FOR CIVILIZATION?

WHAT INVENTIONS HAVE COME FROM SPAIN?

WHAT DISCOVERIES IN THE LABORATORY OR IN SCIENTIFIC FIELDS?

THEY HAVE BEEN SO FEW THAT THEY ARE SCARCELY WORTH MENTIONING...

AMONG THE FREEDOM FIGHTERS THAT ADVANCED CUBA'S INDEPENDENCE MOVEMENT WAS A FIGURE IN THE SPANISH-AMERICAN WAR NAMED JOSÉ MARTÍ, ALSO KNOWN FOR HIS ASTONISHING POETRY.

POETRY PLUS PEACE...

MARTÍ IS ONE OF THE MOST ENDURING POETS OF THE SPANISH LANGUAGE. TOGETHER WITH THE NICARAGUAN RUBÉN DARÍO, HE LED AN ARTISTIC MOVEMENT KNOWN AS MODERNISMO. MODERNISMO WAS DEVOTED TO REVITALIZING THE SPANISH LANGUAGE AND IT'S LITERATURE IN THE AMERICAS.

IN FACT, THIS WAS THE FIRST TIME LATIN AMERICAN WRITERS FROM DIFFERENT COUNTRIES SAW EACH OTHER AS PART OF A SINGLE ARTISTIC MOVEMENT.

51

TO COLUMBUS, BY RUBÉN DARÍO AN EXCERPT

DESGRACIADO ALMIRANTE! TU POBRE AMERICA,

TU INDIA VIRGEN Y HERMOSA DE
   SANGRE CÁLIDA
LA PERLA DE TUS SUEÑOS, ES UNA
   HISTERICA
CON CONVULSIVOS NERVIOS Y FRENTE
   PÁLIDA

UN DESASTROSO ESPÍRITU POSEE
   TU TIERRA:
DONDE LA TRIBU UNIDA BLANDIÓ
   SUS MAZAS
HOY SE ENCIENDE ENTRE HERMANOS
   PERPETUA GUERRA,
SE HIEREN Y DESTROZAN LAS
   MISMAS RAZAS.

-------- X --------

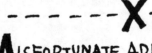

MISFORTUNATE ADMIRAL!
   YOUR POOR AMERICA,
THE BEAUTIFUL INDIAN VIRGIN
   OF HOT BLOOD,
THE PEARL OF YOUR DREAMS, IS A
   HYSTERIC WITH CONVULSIVE
   NERVES AND PALE BROW.

THE STONE IDOL HAS BEEN REPLACED
BY AN ENTHRONED IDOL OF FLESH,
AND EACH DAY THE WHITE DAWN
   ILLUMINATES
ON BLOOD AND ASHES THE FRATERNAL
   BATTLE FIELDS

A RESTLESS, CREATIVE, AND COMMITTED MAN, MARTÍ WAS BORN IN HAVANA IN 1853. HE WAS OFTEN DEPORTED, IMPRISONED, AND FORCED TO HARD LABOR BECAUSE OF HIS POLITICAL IDEAS. HE LIVED IN SPAIN, NEW YORK AND FLORIDA IN THE UNITED STATES AND TRAVELED TO MEXICO, CENTRAL AMERICA, THE DOMINICAN REPUBLIC AND JAMAICA. FOR MANY YEARS HE WORKED AS A CORRESPONDENT FOR VARIOUS NEWSPAPERS LIKE **LA NACIÓN** IN BUENOS AIRES, AND THE <u>NEW YORK SUN</u>. AS A JOURNALIST, HE REPORTED NATURAL DISASTERS, BUT ALSO POLITICAL AND SOCIAL EVENTS, AND HIS REPORTS WERE FILLED WITH COMPASSION. HE DIED IN BATTLE IN 1895

IN 1882, MARTÍ SETTLED IN NEW YORK AND FOUND THE FREEDOM TO WRITE HE HAD ALWAYS LONGED FOR IN HIS HOMELAND. MARTÍ WAS A PROLIFIC WRITER: HIS <u>COMPLETE WORKS</u> FILL 32 VOLUMES.

A SEGMENT OF MARTÍS FAMOUS POEM, **"DOS PATRIAS,"** ABOUT "THE TWO CUBAS" HE SENSED HE HAD IN EXILE.

BAH... A POOR TRANSLATION. BETTER READ IT IN SPANISH.

BUT SOME OF OUR READERS DON'T READ SPANISH...

WELL, THEY SHOULD. DON'T YOU THINK?

WHERE'S THE AUTHOR?

POETRY, SHMOETRY.

Dos Patrias

I have two fatherlands: Cuba and the night.
Or are they one and the same?
As soon as the sun withdraws
Its majesty, with long veils
And a carnation in her hand, silently
Cuba appears to me like a sad widow.
I know what that bloody carnation is
That trembles in her hand! Empty
My breast, destroyed and empty
Where once was my heart.

--------------------X--------------------

Dos patrias tengo yo: Cuba y la noche.
¿O son una las dos? No bien retira
Su majestad el sol, con largos velos
Y un clavel en la mano, silenciosa
Cuba cual viuda triste me aparece.
¡Yo sé cuál es ese clavel sangriento
Que en la mano le tiembla! Está vacío
Mi pecho, destrozado está y vacío
En donde estaba el corazón.

54

REPORTS OF THE WAR WERE FREQUENT IN THE AMERICAN PRESS. AT FIRST, THE PERCEPTION OF CUBA IN POLITICAL CIRCLES AND THE MEDIA IN THE UNITED STATES WAS POSITIVE.

THE CLYDE OHIO ENTERPRISE
— MAY 10, 1895 —
CUBAN REBELS RAPIDLY BECOMING DISCOURAGED

MAY 14, 1896
MANY INSURGENTS KILLED

JAN 21 1897   25¢
THEY ARE PROUD OF IT
SPANIARDS TALK ABOUT A "GREAT VICTORY" NEAR HAVANA

A BRUTAL SLAUGHTER

IT WAS YELLOW JOURNALISM, OF COURSE.

THE CUBAN FREEDOM FIGHTERS WERE EQUATED WITH GEORGE WASHINGTON AND THE AMERICAN REBELS FIGHTING FOR INDEPENDENCE IN 1776: INEXPERIENCED BUT HEROIC, GENUINE IN THEIR STRUGGLE FOR FREEDOM. BUT AS SPAIN RECEDED AND THE OPPORTUNITY TO TAKE CONTROL BECAME APPARENT, THE CUBAN REBELS BEGAN TO BE PORTRAYED AS BARBARIC AND INSUPPORTABLE.

ROUGH RIDERS RECRUITMENT ROOM

IF YOU HATE GREASERS, YOU'LL LOVE THE ROUGH RIDERS!

SIGN UP

FUTURE PRESIDENT THEODORE ROOSEVELT ORGANIZED THE ROUGH RIDERS. THE SQUADRON HAD ALREADY HAD AN ACTIVE ROLE IN THE SOUTHWEST, CRUSHING MEXICAN REBELLIONS. HE TOOK HIS "YANKEES" TO CUBA WHERE THEY FOUGHT THE FAMOUS BATTLE OF SANTIAGO

HIS DISPATCHES STORIES AND PERSONAL NARRATIVES ON CUBA ARE FASCINATING.

STEPHEN CRANE 1871-1900

THE AUTHOR OF THE RED BADGE OF COURAGE, WAS A WAR CORRESPONDENT IN THE SPANISH-AMERICAN WAR.

IN HIS MEMOIR THE ROUGH RIDERS, ROOSEVELT CHRONICLED HIS CAVALRY. IT HAD BEEN A BLOODY, MACHO ENTERPRISE, BUT ROOSEVELT CHOSE TO PAINT IT MILDLY. AFTER ALL, HE WOULD SOON RUN FOR PRESIDENT, AND HIS OWN IMMORTALITY - HIS WISDOM, HIS CARING COURAGE, HIS CARING SPIRIT - WAS AT STAKE.

CUBA

"My troopers, for all their roughness and their ferocity in fight, were rather tenderhearted than otherwise, and they helped the poor creatures, especially the women and children, in every way, giving them food and even carrying the children and the burdens borne by the women...Finally a doctor warned us that we must not touch the bundles of the refugees for fear of infection, as disease had broken out and was rife among them. Accordingly, I had to put a stop to these acts of kindness on the part of my men..."

57

58

59

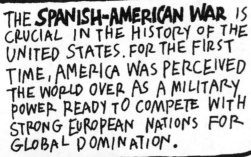

THE **SPANISH-AMERICAN WAR** IS CRUCIAL IN THE HISTORY OF THE UNITED STATES. FOR THE FIRST TIME, AMERICA WAS PERCEIVED THE WORLD OVER AS A MILITARY POWER READY TO COMPETE WITH STRONG EUROPEAN NATIONS FOR GLOBAL DOMINATION.

FOR HISPANICS SOUTH OF THE RIO GRANDE AND IN THE CARIBBEAN SEA, IT WAS CLEAR THAT THE COLOSSAL NORTHERN NEIGHBOR HAD SOUTHBOUND DREAMS OF COLONIALISM.

ENGLAND'S JOHN BULL

WESTERN HEMISPHERE

UNCLE SAM

IN OTHER WORDS, JUST AS SPAIN WAS MOVING OUT, THE UNITED STATES WAS MOVING IN...

NEW YORK

WAS ALREADY A CENTER OF DISSENTING INTELLECTUAL AND POLITICAL DEBATE AT THE END OF THE NINETEENTH CENTURY. IT ATTRACTED POETS, PAINTERS, AND JOURNALISTS, MAINLY FROM SPAIN AND CUBA, BUT ALSO FROM PUERTO RICO. THEY'D MEET FOR TERTULIAS IN CAFES. THE MOST FAMOUS WAS THE SOCIEDAD LITERARIA.

LOCOS
A COMEDY OF GESTURES
-ALFAU-

THESE TERTULIAS WOULD LATER BE IMMORTALIZED BY THE IBERIAN NOVELIST **FELIPE ALFAU,** THE AUTHOR OF **LOCOS: A COMEDY OF GESTURES.** AN EXTRAORDINARY NOVEL ABOUT A GROUP OF SPANISH EMIGRÉS IN NEW YORK TALKING THEIR LIVES AWAY.

SOUNDS LIKE "SEINFELD" EN ESPAÑOL!

I HIGHLY RECOMMEND THIS NOVEL!

¿BUENO, PUES EN QUÉ ESTAMOS? ¿O QUE?

HE MEANS "WELL, SO WHAT'S GOING ON?"

AS A RESULT OF THE WAR, CUBA BECAME A REPUBLIC IN 1898. BUT WAS NOT GRANTED ITS FREEDOM FROM THE U.S. UNTIL 1902. BUT PUERTO RICO WAS CEDED TO THE U.S. SOON ACQUIRING A HYBRID STATUS IN THE INTERNATIONAL COMMUNITY.

IN 1902, ENGLISH WAS DECLARED PUERTO RICO'S SECOND OFFICIAL LANGUAGE. THE END OF THAT DECADE WITNESSED A SUGAR BOOM IN THE ISLAND, THE FORTUITOUS RESULT OF A FREE TRADE AGREEMENT ESTABLISHED BY THE U.S.

GIMME SOME SWEET STUFF!

AZUCAR

INDEPENDENCE FOR CUBA WAS ONLY A MIRAGE. U.S. MILITARY OCCUPATION LASTED UNTIL 1902, WHEN THE ISLAND...

CUBA

...BECAME A SOVEREIGN STATE. IN 1901 THE CUBAN GOVERNMENT ACCEPTED THE PLATT AMENDMENT, GRANTING WASHINGTON THE RIGHT OF INTERVENTION.

63

NEW MEXICO BECAME PART OF THE UNITED STATES IN 1848 WHEN THE TREATY OF GUADALUPE HIDALGO WAS SIGNED, BUT IT WASN'T UNTIL 1912 THAT IT ACQUIRED STATEHOOD.

FELLOW CITIZENS, I UNDERSTAND THAT SOME PEOPLE ARE AFRAID OF THE EXPENSE AND RESPONSIBILITY ATTACHED TO OUR BECOMING A STATE. BUT SUCH FEARS ARE UNWORTHY OF AMERICAN MANHOOD! IF THEY WERE TO PREVAIL IN THE ORDINARY AFFAIRS OF LIFE NO ONE WOULD EXERCISE HIS RIGHTS OF CITIZENSHIP, OR INCUR THE DUTIES AND RESPONSIBILITIES OF FAMILY LIFE.

MIGUEL ANTONIO OTERO, ONE OF THE FIRST INSTITUTIONALIZED LATINO POLITICAL LEADERS, WAS GOVERNOR BETWEEN 1897 and 1906. DURING HIS TENURE HE PUSHED FOR STATEHOOD. IN 1940, ALREADY A VERY OLD MAN, HE PUBLISHED A MEMOIR MY NINE YEARS AS GOVERNOR OF THE TERRITORY OF NEW MEXICO.

NEW MEXICO

IN 1910, THE MEXICAN REVOLUTION BROKE OUT..., AND ITS REPERCUSSIONS FOR THE U.S., AND IN PARTICULAR FOR LATINOS, WERE IMMENSE.

...WHICH, BY THE WAY, WAS THE FIRST ARMED SOCIAL MOVEMENT OF THE TWENTIETH CENTURY, PRECEDING THE SOVIET REVOLUTION OF 1917, AND WORLD WAR I.

DICTATOR PORFIRIO DÍAZ HAD RULED MEXICO FOR OVER THIRTY-FIVE YEARS. HE HAD BROUGHT POLITICAL STABILITY AND AN EXPANSION OF ECONOMIC MARKETS, AND HE HAD BUILT THE RAILROAD SYSTEM. HIS REGIME HAD BROUGHT THE NATION INTO THE MODERN ERA, BUT AT THE EXPENSE OF A WIDE SEGMENT OF THE POPULATION, PARTICULARLY IN THE COUNTRYSIDE.

65

THE REVOLUTIONARY HEROES **PANCHO VILLA** AND **EMILIANO ZAPATA**, EACH ON HIS OWN AND THEN JOINTLY, BATTLED DÍAZ'S DICTATORSHIP. THE RESULT WAS A STATE OF POLITICAL ANARCHY THAT LASTED ALMOST THE ENTIRE DECADE.

AMONG THE EVENTS THAT PRECIPITATED THE MEXICAN REVOLUTION WAS A BLOODY STRIKE, IN 1906, IN THE **CANANEA COPPER MINES** OWNED BY U.S. COMPANIES, NEAR THE MEXICAN BORDER WITH ARIZONA. THIS STRIKE WAS FOLLOWED BY ANOTHER IN RIO BLANCO, VERACRUZ. IN BOTH, DÍAZ'S SOLDIERS KILLED MANY WORKERS. AND THE MESSAGE WAS LOUD AND CLEAR: MEXICO'S RULING REGIME SIDED WITH THE UNITED STATES.

SO THE REVOLUTIONARIES THAT OPPOSED DÍAZ ALSO FOUGHT AGAINST THE "HIDDEN INTERVENTION OF THE U.S. IN MEXICO."

ABOUT A FOURTH OF THE U.S. ARMY WAS "ON CALL" AT THE BORDER MEXICAN REBELS, LIKE VILLA, OCCASIONALLY WENT NORTHBOUND AND FOUGHT ON THE AMERICAN SIDE OF THE BORDER, AS IN THE FAMOUS BATTLE OF COLUMBUS, NEW MEXICO.

MILLIONS OF WOMEN JOINED THE ARMY ON THE BATTLEFIELD. THEY WERE KNOWN AS **LAS SOLDADERAS** - FEMALE CADETS. THEIR EFFORTS EVEN INSPIRED SONGS, SUCH AS "LA ADELITA."

La Güera y su gente
improvisa sus trincheras;
aunque es mujer
tiene el grado
de coronel; y sus trenzas
no han impedido
que ostente
con orgullo sus estrellas.

The blondie and her people
improvise a makeshift trench;
even though she is a woman
her rank is colonel;
and her braids don't
get in the way
of her insignias.

¡VÁMONOS, MI AMOR!

IRONICALLY, IMMIGRATION OF MEXICAN CAMPESINOS TO THE UNITED STATES INTENSIFIED AROUND 1890. STATISTICS ARE SKETCHY, BUT THOUSANDS OF ILEGALES MADE IT TO EL NORTE ATTRACTED BY LOW WAGES BUT PLENTIFUL OPPORTUNITIES. THE MEXICAN REVOLUTION FUELED MASS MIGRATIONS UNTIL AROUND 1930.

THOSE WERE ALSO THE DECADES OF MASSIVE IMMIGRATION OF EASTERN EUROPEAN IMMIGRANTS TO THE UNITED STATES. AS MANY AS 22 MILLION PEOPLE ENTERED THE COUNTRY AT THE TIME, FORCING WASHINGTON TO VIRTUALLY CLOSE THE BORDERS IN 1924 THROUGH THE REED-JOHNSON ACT. BUT THE BAN DID NOT APPLY TO NATIONS OF THE WESTERN HEMISPHERE, SO THE MEXICAN ESPALDAS MOJADAS KEPT ON TRAVELLING NORTHBOUND.

MMM... BEN + JERRYS

ELLIS ISLAND

MMM... ESPALDA MOJADA. IT MEANS "WETBACK" (A SLUR TO MOST...)

DO YOU KNOW WHY THEY WERE CALLED BY THAT NAME? THEY CROSSED WHEN NO ONE COULD SEE THEM.

THE HEROES OF THE MEXICAN REVOLUTION - VILLA AND ZAPATA ESPECIALLY - BECAME LEGENDARY AMONG MEXICAN-AMERICANS. THEY APPEAR IN NUMEROUS MURALS, OIL PAINTINGS, POEMS, PLAYS AND NOVELS. AND EACH HAS SEVERAL CORRIDOS RECOUNTING THEIR ADVENTURES. ALSO POPULAR IN THE SOUTHWEST IS THE VIRGEN DE GUADALUPE, THE PATRON MOTHER OF MODERN MEXICO.

TIERRA O MUERTE

PANCHO VILLA
EL CENTAURO DEL NORTE

LA VIRGEN DE GUADALUPE

TACOS LA LUPITA

MEXICANS CALL THEMSELVES GUADALUPANOS.

VIRGIN APPARITION

JUAN DIEGO

69

MIRROR, MIRROR, ON THE WALL, WHO'S THE FAIREST OF US ALL?

PERHAPS THE MOST DISTINGUISHED ARTIST TO EMERGE FROM THE MEXICAN REVOLUTION WAS **JOSE GUADALUPE POSADA.** HE WAS AN ENGRAVER WHOSE POPULAR ETCHINGS MADE INEXPENSIVELY AND REFLECTING MAJOR HISTORICAL AND NATURAL EVENTS, SERVED AS AN INVALUABLE WINDOW TO THESE TURBULENT TIMES.

POSADA WAS MY PROGENITOR, HE TURNED THE **CALAVERA,** A MEXICAN POP CHARACTER, INTO A NATIONAL ICON, EQUAL IN STATURE TO UNCLE SAM.

PERHAPS YOU WOULD HAVE LOOKED A LITTLE BETTER HAD POSADA HIMSELF DONE THE JOB.

TRY PLASTIC SURGERY.

LaLo. panchito Chava ILan

EACH NOVEMBER, MEXICANS AND MEXICAN-AMERICANS CELEBRATE THE DAY OF THE DEAD BY SPENDING TIME IN CEMETERIES AT THE TOMB OF THEIR BELOVED DECEASED. THEY EAT LUNCH SING AND REMINISCE, AND EVEN SPEND THE NIGHT.

THE **DIA DE LOS MUERTOS** IS THE MOST IMPORTANT HOLIDAY FOR MANY CHICANOS, WIDELY CELEBRATED AND NOT ALTOGETHER "DISTORTED" BY CONSUMERISM — IN TEXAS, NEW MEXICO, ARIZONA AND CALIFOIRNIA.

THE SUCCESSORS OF JOSE GUADALUPE POSADA WERE THE MEMBERS OF AN INTERNATIONAL ARTISTIC MOVEMENT. KNOWN AS **MURALISMO.** IT WAS LEAD BY THREE MAJOR PAINTERS:

ART FOR THE PEOPLE!

¡VIVA LA REVOLUCION!

RIVERA

OROZCO

SIQUEIROS

THEIR VIEWS WERE MARXIST TO VARIOUS DEGREES AND THEIR GOAL WAS TO MAKE ART A TOOL FOR SOCIAL CHANGE. THEY PAINTED MURALS ALL OVER MEXICO THAT DEPICTED THE STRUGGLE OF MEXICANS TO BE THE SOLE OWNERS OF THEIR DESTINY.

THEY WERE ALSO COMMISSIONED BY WEALTHY AMERICAN ENTREPRENEURS TO MAKE MURALS IN THE UNITED STATES - IN POMONA COLLEGE, AT DARTMOUTH COLLEGE, AND AT NEW YORK'S ROCKEFELLER CENTER AMONG MANY OTHER PLACES.

OROZCO WAS THE MOST RADICAL OF THE THREE. HIS COMMUNIST VIEWS MADE HIM A DISSENTER AMONG LEFT-WING INTELLECTUALS. HE WAS OFTEN IN PRISON AND FORCED TO LEAVE MEXICO. WHEN LEON TROTSKY SOUGHT EXILE IN MEXICO AFTER A FEUD WITH LENIN, OROZCO NOT ONLY FOUGHT UNSUC-CESSFULLY AS IT TURNED OUT, TO CLOSE THE NATIONS DOORS TO HIM, BUT WAS ALSO INVOLVED IN AN ASSAS SINATION ATTEMPT.

71

FRIDA KAHLO, THE DAUGHTER OF A JEWISH PHOTOGRAPHER FROM HUNGARY, WAS RIVERA'S WIFE AND A WORLD-RENOWNED PAINTER. SHE WAS ALSO A MARXIST. BUT HER PAINTINGS ARE VERY DIFFERENT FROM THOSE OF THE <u>MURALISTAS</u>- THEY WERE INTIMATE, SELF-OBSESSED. IN FACT, RATHER THAN PORTRAY EPIC EVENTS IN HER ART, KAHLO SPENT HER DAYS CRAFTING SELF-PORTRAITS.

SHE HAD SUFFERED A TERRIBLE STREETCAR ACCIDENT AT AN EARLY AGE AND WAS PHYSICALLY HANDICAPPED FOR THE REST OF HER LIFE. SHE NEVER HAD CHILDREN AND DIED YOUNG, BUT HER ART BECAME A SYMBOL OF WOMEN'S LIBERATION. CHICANAS DURING THE CHICANO MOVEMENT EMBRACED HER AS THE SUPREME ICON.

BY 1929, WHEN THE STOCK MARKET COLLAPSED AND THE DEPRESSION BEGAN, A NEW SPIRIT OF NATIONALISM HAD INVADED THE HISPANIC WORLD

PAN AM EXPRESS

IT WAS A SPIRIT OF COMRADESHIP, OF UNITY AGAINST THE MENACING U.S. FOREIGN POLICIES.

A MYTH BEGAN TO FLOURISH IN THE MEXICAN-AMERICAN SOUL— THE LEGEND OF **AZTLÁN.** ACCORDING TO THIS LEGEND, MEXICAN-AMERICANS DON'T DESCEND FROM MEXICO, BUT THE OTHER WAY AROUND.

WELCOME BACK AZTLÁN

FUTURE SITE OF TENOCHTITLÁN

CHICANOS IN THE 1950'S AND 1960'S CALLED THEMSELVES "**LA RAZA**" AND "THE PEOPLE OF AZTLÁN." AZTLÁN IS THE CHICANO HOMELAND— HOME OF LA RAZA. MEXICAN HISTORY SAYS THE AZTECS FOUNDED THE NATION'S CAPITAL, TENOCHTITLÁN, TODAY'S <u>DISTRITO FEDERAL</u>.

THEIR PROPHESIES HAD ESTABLISHED THAT THE SITE WOULD BE RECOGNIZED BY SIGHTING A HUGE LAKE WITH AN EAGLE SOMEWHERE IN THE MIDDLE PERCHED ON A CACTUS WHILE DEVOURING A SNAKE.

WE ARE LA RAZA CÓSMICA!

VASCONCELOS

CHICANO POWER

73

WE IN THE AMERICAS ARE BY NATURE DREAMERS.

NOTHING WRONG WITH THAT!

JOSE ENRIQUE RODÓ

WAS AN URUGUAYAN INTELLECTUAL. IN 1900 HE PUBLISHED A BOOK TITLED **ARIEL.** IN IT HE ARGUES THAT THE YOUTH IN LATIN AMERICA NEEDED TO FIND THEIR OWN CHARACTER, THEIR OWN ROAD TO SUCCESS, AND NOT TO IMITATE THE UNITED STATES BLINDLY. RODÓ ALSO WROTE THAT WHEN COMPARED TO NORTH AMERICA'S MATERIALISM, LATIN AMERICA WAS MUCH MORE "SPIRITUAL."

THEN IN **1925, JOSÉ VASCONCELOS** MEXICO'S MINISTER OF EDUCATION AND A PROMOTER OF THE MURALIST ART OF RIVERA, OROZCO AND SIQUEIROS, WROTE HIS FAMOUS INTRODUCTORY ESSAY TO **LA RAZA CÓSMICA.**

THE COSMIC RACE.

VASCONCELOS' ARGUMENT PROVED TO BE EXTRAORDINARILY INFLUENTIAL ESPECIALLY AMONG CHICANOS.

HE CLAIMED THAT **MESTIZOS** A MIXTURE OF IBERIANS AND ABORIGINALS IN MESO AMERICA, WHICH HE CALLED "THE COSMIC RACE," WERE CALLED TO CONQUER THE GLOBE IN THE NEAR FUTURE. THEIR "ADAPTABILITY", THEIR HYBRIDITY, HE WROTE, WAS A FORMULA FOR SUCCESS.

74

RICARDO AND ENRIQUE FLORES MAGÓN WERE SYNDICALISTS FROM MEXICO WHO IN THE FIRST DECADE OF THE 20th CENTURY SOUGHT ASYLUM IN THE UNITED STATES. THEY WERE LATER CONDEMNED FOR TREASON. THEY ARE FAMOUS FOR PUBLISHING A MAGAZINE, **REGENERACIÓN**, WHICH FOSTERED A CALL TO ACTION REGARDING THE IMPOVERISHED STATUS OF MEXICANS SOUTH OF THE RIO GRANDE.

SOME YEARS LATER, THE NEWSPAPERS EL HERALDO AND LA OPINIÓN ACQUIRED A SOLID READERSHIP AND SERVED AS A BRIDGE BETWEEN DISCONNECTED COMMUNITIES IN THE SOUTHWEST.

A SYNDICALIST IS A UNION MEMBER.

WHERE NEWSPAPERS AND <u>CORRIDOS</u> DIDN'T DO THE JOB OF INFORMING PEOPLE, WE ACTORS DID. OUR TROUPES WANDERED ACROSS THE NATION TO SPANISH-SPEAKING COMMUNITIES. WE WOULD OFTEN TRANSFORM MAJOR NEWS EVENTS INTO PLAYS FILLED WITH COMEDY AND USEFUL KNOWLEDGE.

TREASURE ISLAND

FINE CIGARS

TABACOS **FAD** 5¢

IN THE NORTHEAST, A FLUX OF PUERTO RICAN WORKERS, MAINLY FROM THE TOBACCO INDUSTRY, HAD MOVED TO NEW YORK AND BEGAN LABORING IN FACTORIES.

WE DON'T NEED YOU ANYMORE!

YOU'RE TAKING AWAY OUR JOBS!

¡LA PINCHE SUERTE!

RACISM WAS RAMPANT!

WASN'T IT ALWAYS?

BERNARDO VEGA, A TOBACCO WORKER, ARRIVED IN NEW YORK CITY IN 1916. IN HIS **MEMOIRS**, HE CHRONICLED THE PLIGHT OF PUERTO RICANS.

THE IMAGE OF PUERTO RICANS AS ILLITERATE IS AN ABERRATION. IN OUR FACTORY, PUERTO RICANS WERE ALWAYS READING: ZOLA, DUMAS, FLAUBERT, JULES VERNE... WE ALSO FOUGHT FOR BETTER CONDITIONS FOR ALL WORKERS.

THE VICIOUS CIRCLE OF POVERTY THAT ENTRAPPED THE PUERTO RICAN POPULATION IN THE NORTHEAST WAS THE RESULT OF THE POLITICAL SITUATION IN PUERTO RICO. NO SOONER DID THE SPANISH COLONIAL PRESENCE DISAPPEAR AT THE TURN OF THE CENTURY THAN PUERTO RICO WAS QUICKLY OVERWHELMED BY THE U.S.

PUERTO RICO IS KNOWN AS BORINQUÉN, AND ITS PEOPLE AS LOS BORICUAS.

BORINQUÉN MEANS "LAND OF THE BRAVE LORD." THIS WAS WHAT THE ARAWAK INDIANS CALLED THEIR ISLAND BEFORE THE SPANIARDS ARRIVED.

LIBERTAD BORINQUEÑA

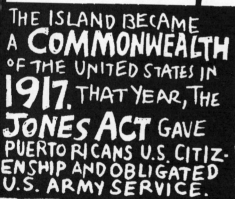

AZUCAR

IN 1932, THE SUGAR BOOM COLLAPSED AND MASSIVE WAVES OF PUERTO RICAN IMMIGRANTS BEGAN TO MOVE TO NEW YORK. THIS TREND WOULD PEAK IN 1945.

THE ISLAND BECAME A **COMMONWEALTH** OF THE UNITED STATES IN **1917.** THAT YEAR, THE **JONES ACT** GAVE PUERTO RICANS U.S. CITIZENSHIP AND OBLIGATED U.S. ARMY SERVICE.

U$ BUSINESS

PUERTO RICO'S STATUS AS A NO MAN'S LAND, NEITHER FULLY CARIBBEAN NOR FULLY AMERICAN, BEGAN...

MANY PUERTO RICANS LEFT. THE MAJORITY WERE POOR **JÍBAROS,** PEASANTS FROM THE COUNTRYSIDE LOOKING FOR BETTER JOB OPPORTUNITIES, BUT MIDDLE- AND UPPER- MIDDLE CLASS PEOPLE ALSO CROSSED THE CHANNEL.

IN SPITE OF THE JONES ACT AND THE STATUS OF PUERTO RICO, THE DRIVE FOR ITS INDEPENDENCE HAS REMAINED UNABATED SINCE THE TIMES OF **JOSÉ DE DIEGO**, A NINETEENTH CENTURY PUERTO RICAN POET.

DE DIEGO WROTE THE POEM "TO THE PERSECUTED" TO EXPRESS HIS INDEPENDISTA SPIRIT.

RESURGE, BREATHE, SHOUT, WALK, FIGHT, VIBRATE, GLIDE, THUNDER, SHINE FORTH...

DO AS THE RIVER RICH WITH NEW RAINWATER:

GROW.

OR LIKE THE SEA APPROACHING A ROCKY SHORE:

STRIKE.

PEDRO ALBIZU CAMPOS, PUERTO RICO'S MOST PROMINENT INDEPENDENTISTA WAS HEAD OF THE **PUERTO RICAN NATIONALIST PARTY.** HERE HE IS, ADDRESSING THE ASSOCIATED PRESS IN 1936.

"SIXTY-EIGHT YEARS AGO, OUR REPUBLIC WAS FORMED. ON **SEPTEMBER 23, 1868**, WE DECLARED OUR INDEPENDENCE FROM SPAIN. PUERTO RICO WAS RICH IN NAME AND IN SOIL. OUR CHRISTIAN FOUNDATION CREATED A FAMILY MODEL THAT WAS TO BE A VANGUARD OF MODERN CIVILIZATION... WHAT DO WE HAVE WHEN WE HAVE NOTHING BUT DEPENDENCY ON THOSE WHO DESTROYED US?... OUR OWN PEOPLE SEE PUERTO RICAN NATIONALISM AS NOTHING BUT A PATH OF TERRORISM AND MURDER, BUT THEY DEFEAT OUR SPIRIT IN DENOUNCING THEMSELVES."

80

THE SENTIMENTS OF **ALBIZU CAMPOS** AND HIS NATIONALIST COLLEAGUES COMPRISE ONLY ONE SIDE OF THE COIN IN PUERTO RICO'S POLITICAL STRUGGLES. THE OTHER SIDE EMBRACED THE COMMON WEALTH STATUS AND SUPPORTED AN ONGOING ALLIANCE WITH THE U.S. IN 1948 **LUIS MUÑOZ MARÍN** BECAME THE ISLAND'S FIRST ELECTED GOVERNOR AND REMAINED IN OFFICE UNTIL 1964. HE SHUNNED INDEPENDENTISMO AND PROMOTED U.S. TIES TO THE PUERTO RICAN CITIZENRY.

IN 1920, IT WAS ESTIMATED THAT ONLY 12,000 PUERTO RICANS LIVED ON THE U.S. MAINLAND. IN 1945, THE NUMBER REACHED 100,000. BUT AFTER WORLD WAR II, THE BORICUA POPULATION IN EXILE INCREASED DRAMATICALLY, ESPECIALLY IN MANHATTAN AND ITS NEIGHBORING BOROUGHS.

Yo ♥ NUEBA YOL

PUERTO RICANS QUICKLY "ETHNICIZED" THEIR NEW ENVIRONMENT, ADAPTING IT TO THEIR NEEDS, AND BRINGING A DIFFERENT LIGHT AND FLAVOR TO ITS STREETS AND RESTAURANTS. EAST HARLEM BECAME SPANISH HARLEM. OTHER PUERTO RICANS SETTLED DOWN IN THE SOUTH BRONX AND THROUGHOUT THE LOWER EAST SIDE IN MANHATTAN.

PUES CHICO, ARE WE IN PUERTO RICO OR **NUEBA YOL**?

AY MUJER, I CAN'T TELL THE DIFFERENCE!

BODEGA

THE **LOWER EAST SIDE** HAD BEEN A PREDOMINANTLY JEWISH NEIGHBORHOOD. PUERTO RICANS RENAMED IT, IN SPANGLISH— THE MIXED LANGUAGE OF SPANISH AND ENGLISH— **LOISAIDA.**

SINCE PUERTO RICANS WERE U.S. CITIZENS BY BIRTH, THEY WERE ENTITLED TO LEGAL BENEFITS AND PROTECTION AND NOT SUBJECTED TO DEPORTATION.

PASSPORT US

PÚM!

AT THE END OF OCTOBER, 1950, THERE WAS A PUERTO RICAN TERRORIST ATTACK AT THE **BLAIR HOUSE** IN WASHINGTON, D.C., WHILE PRESIDENT HARRY TRUMAN WAS IN OFFICE.
TWO PEOPLE WERE KILLED AND THREE WOUNDED. THE INCIDENT DREW GLOBAL ATTENTION TO PUERTO RICAN NATIONALISM.

A FEW YEARS LATER, IN MARCH 1954, FOUR PUERTO RICAN INDEPENDENTISTAS-INCLUDING RAFAEL CANDEL MIRANDA, ANDRES CORDERO, AND LOLITA LEBRÓN-TRIED TO ASSASINATE PRESIDENT HARRY S. TRUMAN. THE PRESIDENT WAS NOT INJURED, BUT THREE CONGRESSMEN WERE. THE "TERRORISTS" WERE CAPTURED, SENT TO PRISON, AND NOT RELEASED UNTIL 1979.

A MESSAGE FROM GOD IN THE ATOMIC AGE
I. VILAR

LOLITA LEBRON'S GRAND-DAUGHTER, IRENE VILAR, WROTE A FAMILY MEMOIR ABOUT THE "INTIMATE" AFTERMATH OF THE EVENT.

eeek

DID THEY SAY "VIVA MEXICO?"!

THE PEOPLE OF PUERTO RICO ARE PROFOUNDLY INDIGNANT AT THE ATTEMPT MADE AT BLAIR HOUSE, IN WHICH TWO PUERTO RICAN NATIONALISTS WERE INVOLVED. WE WOULD FEEL ASHAMED OF CALLING OURSELVES PUERTO RICANS, IF IT WERE NOT FOR THE FACT THAT THE NATIONALIST GANGSTERS ARE LESS THAN 500 IN NUMBER, AMONG THE MORE THAN 2 MILLION DECENT, DEMOCRACY-LOVING AMERICAN CITIZENS THAT MAKE UP OUR COMMUNITY."

GOVERNOR LUIS MUÑOZ MARIN'S TELEVISED SPEECH

A BIT EARLIER, HISTORIAN **HERBERT EUGENE BOLTON** BEGAN TO CALL ATTENTION TO THE HISPANIC CONTRIBUTION IN U.S. HISTORY AND CULTURE. IN <u>THE SPANISH BORDERLANDS: A CHRONICLE OF OLD FLORIDA AND THE SOUTHWEST</u>, PUBLISHED IN 1921, HE STRESSED THE HEROIC SPIRIT OF THE SPANISH EXPLORERS AND SETTLERS. IN SUBSEQUENT DECADES, BOLTON'S WORK REEVALUATED THE MISIÓN AS A "FRONTIER INSTITUTE" IN THE SPANISH-AMERICAN COLONIES.

SCAREAMOUNT PICTURES PRESENTS

DIRECTED BY BIGG AUTRY
PRODUCED BY HAY TREAD

FROM THE MAKERS OF "THE MEXTRATERRESTIAL" AND "BROWNZILLA" IT'S

DESPITE THIS APPROACH, HISPANOPHOBIA PREVAILED. MANY HISTORIANS, SUCH AS CAREY McWILLIAMS, WOULD GLORIFY THE SPANISH HERITAGE IN THE SOUTHWEST BUT MINIMIZE THE MEXICAN INFLUENCE AND PRESENCE.

HOW'S ABOUT A LITTLE BESITO, MARIA?

HISPANOPHOBIA
YOU WILL FEEL HIS-PANIC!

MOVIES CONFORM AND DEFORM IDEAS AND ATTITUDES. TAKE THE CASE OF JOHN WAYNE AS A MOVIE CHARACTER: THE ALL AMERICAN HERO, THE BIGOTED HATER OF MEXICANS AND INDIANS. HE SPENT HIS CAREER DOING WESTERNS, KILLING ANY DARKSKINNED CREATURE. IN REAL LIFE HE HAD THREE HISPANIC WIVES...

THE SPANISH BORDERLANDS: A CHRONICLE OF OLD FLORIDA AND THE SOUTHWEST

MEANWHILE

AFRICANA

ARTHUR A. SCHOMBURG WAS AMONG THE MOST ILLUSTRIOUS MEMBERS OF THE HARLEM RENAISSANCE. HE WAS BORN IN PUERTO RICO AND HIS MOTHER WAS FROM ST. THOMAS. HE ARRIVED IN NEW YORK IN 1891 AND HELPED PROMOTE THE INDEPENDENCE OF CUBA AND PUERTO RICO. WITH TIME, HE WOULD BECOME AN IMPORTANT ESSAYIST.

BUT HIS REAL FAME WAS THE RESULT OF HIS HUNGER FOR COLLECTING BOOKS: WHEN HE DIED, SCHOMBURG HAD GATHERED THOUSANDS OF BOOKS AND MANUSCRIPTS OF AFRICANA WHICH HAVE BEEN INCREDIBLY USEFUL IN UNDERSTANDING AFRICAN AMERICAN HISTORY AND CULTURE.

HE ALSO WROTE IN THE AMERICAN GRAIN, WHICH ADDRESSES THE SPANISH HERITAGE OF THE U.S.

"MUSIC AND PAINTINGS AND ALL THAT THAT'S ALL THEY THOUGHT OF IN PUERTO RICO IN THE OLD SPANISH DAYS WHEN SHE WAS A GIRL."

YOU SEE THAT DOCTOR? HE'S THE GREAT **WILLIAM CARLOS WILLIAMS**, A POET OF ENORMOUS POWER WHOSE MOTHER WAS PUERTO RICAN.

IN HIS AUTOBIOGRAPHY, PUBLISHED IN 1951, HE DISCUSSED HIS CONNECTION TO THE ISLAND.

85

IN THE THIRTIES, RADIO STATIONS IN SPANISH BEGAN TO EMERGE LIKE MUSHROOMS AFTER THE RAIN. AND SO DID MOVIES DUBBED IN SPANISH. IT WAS CLEAR THAT A SEGMENT OF THE POPULATION WAS LOYAL TO THE LANGUAGE, REFUSING TO GIVE IT UP WHILE LEARNING ENGLISH

1931

THE THIRTIES BROUGHT THE **DEPRESSION** AND **WORLD WAR II**. ALL ACROSS THE COUNTRY MOST LATINOS WERE LIVING IN MISERABLE CONDITIONS, ISOLATED IN GHETTOES...

...BUT THERE WAS TRANSGRESSION IN THE AIR...

... AND INDEED, NO SOONER DID THE THIRTIES END, THAN A NUMBER OF RIOTS MADE BIG NEWS.

(school time)

DURING WORLD WAR II, THE U.S. ARMY RECRUITED HALF A MILLION MEXICAN-AMERICANS. THEY FOUGHT IN THE SOUTH PACIFIC, IN ITALY, FRANCE, AND GERMANY. BUT BACK AT HOME, THE **PACHUCOS**, YOUTHS OF MEXICAN DESCENT LIVING IN BARRIOS IN CALIFORNIA, WERE PERCEIVED AS A THREAT.

1942: THE SLEEPY LAGOON INCIDENT IN LOS ANGELES

THAT'S BECAUSE THEY SAW THEMSELVES AS "STEP-CHILDREN OF THE NATION," NOT FULL-FLEDGED CITIZENS.

THEIR WAY OF WALKING, OF DRESSING, OF THINKING WAS DIFFERENT.

CON SAFOS

¡DEJAME EN PAZ!

I'LL LEAVE YOU IN PIECES NOT IN PEACE!

DEFENDANTS IN THE SLEEPY LAGOON CASE

THE SLEEPY LAGOON RIOT TOOK PLACE IN LOS ANGELES. ON AUGUST 2, 1942, JOSÉ DÍAZ, A CHICANO, WAS FOUND DEAD ON A DIRT ROAD NOT FAR FROM HIS HOUSE. THE NIGHT BEFORE, A GANG OF CHICANOS, KNOWN AS THE 38TH ST. CLUB, HAD CLASHED WITH ANOTHER GANG. THE LAPD THREW THE WHOLE GANG IN JAIL. IT WAS A CASE OF OVERT RACISM. THE ENGLISH SPEAKING PRESS PORTRAYED THE MEXICANS AS "HOODLUMS," DESCRIBING THEM AS A PEOPLE WITH A THIRST FOR VIOLENCE STEMMING FROM THEIR AZTEC ANCESTRY.

THE GANG MEMBERS'S SENTENCES, DELIVERED IN JANUARY 1943, RANGED FROM ASSAULT TO FIRST DEGREE MURDER. EVENTUALLY, THE SECOND DISTRICT COURT OF APPEALS REVERSED THE VERDICT, CALLING THE EVIDENCE INSUBSTANTIAL. THE INCIDENT INCREASED THE TENSION BETWEEN ANGLOS AND CHICANOS.

IN THE SPRING OF **1943**, ANOTHER RIOT OCURRED, THE SO CALLED **ZOOT SUIT RIOT**.

THIS FIGHT STARTED WITH A GROUP OF U.S. MARINES + SAILORS FROM OAKLAND BEATING BLACKS + MEXICAN-AMERICANS WHILE THE POLICE WATCHED AND DID NOTHING. THEN, POLICE ARRESTED THE CHICANOS, ACCUSING THEM OF DISTURBING THE PEACE.

THE **ZOOT SUIT** WAS THE DRESS STYLE WORN BY THE PACHUCOS.

¡TEN CABRÓN!

ME LA VAS A PAGAR...

IN JUNE 1943, A GROUP OF CHICANOS BEAT ANGLO SAILORS WHO WERE TRYING TO PICK UP SOME CHICANAS. THEY WERE ARRESTED BY THE POLICE, BUT THAT SAME NIGHT THE SAILORS ENTERED THE CARMEN THEATER AND BEAT THE MEXICAN ZOOT-SUITERS.

THE CLASHES SKYROCKETED, AND ON

JUNE 7, MOBS WERE RIOTING. CHICANOS, BLACKS, AND FILIPINOS WERE TARGETS IN RESTAURANTS, THEATERS, BARS. SOME 600 CHICANOS WERE ARRESTED. NEWSPAPERS APPLAUDED THE LA POLICE, WHO CLAIMED THE ARRESTS WERE "PREVENTIVE."

THE SITUATION GOT SO BAD, THE AUTHORITIES DECLARED DOWNTOWN LOS ANGELES "OFF LIMITS" FOR SAILORS AND OTHER ARMY PERSONNEL. ¡TOMA!

Los Angeles Daily News

"The time has come to serve notice that the City of Los Angeles will no longer be terrorized by a relatively small handful of morons parading as zoot-suit hoodlums. To delay action now means to court disaster later."

RACISM WAS EVERYWHERE!

TANDO →

ZOOTER ↓

(IN HIS TACUCHE OR TRAPOS)

THE **PACHUCOS** BECAME NOTORIOUS. SOME CONSIDER THEM PRECURSORS TO THE CHICANO ACTIVISTS WHO WOULD EMERGE DURING THE CIVIL RIGHTS ERA.

THE TERM "**CHICANO**" DID NOT BEGIN TO BE USED UNTIL 1947. DOES IT COME FROM MEJICANO?

DRAPE →

OCTAVIO PAZ →

NEITHER MEXICAN NOR AMERICAN, THE PACHUCO IS AN EXTREME, AN ANOMALY, AN EXCEPTION.

TABLITAS

PEGGED

OCTAVIO PAZ, THE MEXICAN POET AND ESSAYIST, LIVED IN LOS ANGELES IN THE LATE 1940'S HIS STAY INSPIRED HIM TO UNDERSTAND THE PACHUCO.

PAZ'S COMMENTS, WHICH BECAME THE FIRST CHAPTER OF HIS CLASSIC 1950 BOOK **THE LABYRINTH OF SOLITUDE** ARE DEROGATORY AND CONDESCENDING!

OH COME ON, THAT'S TOO SIMPLISTIC!

"WHAT DISTINGUISHES [THE PACHUCOS], I THINK, IS THEIR FURTIVE RESTLESS AIR: THEY ACT LIKE PERSONS WHO ARE WEAVING DISGUISES, WHO ARE AFRAID OF A STRANGER'S LOOK BECAUSE IT COULD STRIP THEM AND LEAVE THEM STARK NAKED. WHEN YOU TALK TO THEM, YOU OBSERVE THAT THEIR SENSIBILITIES ARE LIKE A PENDULUM, BUT A PENDULUM THAT HAS LOST ITS REASON AND SWINGS VIOLENTLY AND IRRATIONALLY BACK AND FORTH."

FROM "THE LABYRINTH OF SOLITUDE."

WORLD WAR II ENDED AND SOLDIERS RETURNED HOME IN NEED OF WORK, SO CHEAP LABOR WAS NO LONGER NEEDED AS MUCH AS BEFORE. IN RESPONSE, BETWEEN 1953 AND 1956 THE UNITED STATES GOVERNMENT ORCHESTRATED **OPERATION WETBACK**, IN WHICH MORE THAN TWO MILLION MEXICANS WERE REPATRIATED.

"TO REPATRIATE" IS TO SEND A PERSON BACK TO HIS COUNTRY OF ORIGIN.

WHILE MEXICANS WERE BEATEN AND DISCRIMINATED AGAINST IN THE SOUTHWEST, THEY BEGAN TO APPEAR MORE REGULARLY IN ORGANIZED SPORTS, PARTICULARLY IN BASEBALL.

BASEBALL WAS INTRODUCED INTO THE HISPANIC WORLD BY AMERICAN SAILORS STATIONED IN CENTRAL AMERICA AND THE CARIBBEAN JUST AFTER THE CIVIL WAR.

SO CCER HAS ALWAYS BEEN OUR FAVORITE SPORT!

PERHAPS, BUT NOT EVERYWHERE ON THE CONTINENT. IN FACT, IN CUBA, PUERTO RICO, VENE-ZUELA, PANAMA, AND THE DOMINICAN REPUBLIC, BASEBALL IS MUCH MORE POPULAR THAN SOCCER.

FOR A WHILE, LATINO **PELOTEROS**, LIKE THEIR NEGRO COLLEAGUES, WERE EXCLUDED FROM PROFESSIONAL BASEBALL. MANY OF THEM—LIKE **MARTÍN DIHIGO** AND **CRISTÓBAL "THE CUBAN STRONGMAN" TORRIENTE** — SOUGHT REFUGE IN THE NEGRO LEAGUES. FORTUNATELY THOSE YEARS ARE OVER.

COACH

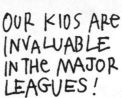

OUR KIDS ARE INVALUABLE IN THE MAJOR LEAGUES!

CHICAGO

IN 1912, ADOLFO LUQUE, A GREAT CUBAN **PELOTERO**, BEGAN HIS DISTINGUISHED 23-YEAR CAREER IN THE U·S· MAJOR LEAGUES.

LUIS APARICIO

IN THE 1950'S, BIG LEAGUE FIGURE **LUIS APARICIO**, ORIGINALLY FROM VENEZUELA, BEGAN A CAREER THAT SAW HIM PLAY A RECORD 2,581 GAMES AS SHORT-STOP. HE WON NINE GOLD GLOVES AND LED THE AMERICAN LEAGUE IN STOLEN BASES FOR 9 STRAIGHT YEARS.

MY HERO!

SAY IT, AIN'T SO, JOE

94

PUERTO RICAN **HALL** OF **FAMER ROBERTO CLEMENTE**

ORLANDO "THE BABY BULL" **CEPEDA**

DOMINICAN STAR JUAN MARICHAL

HEY RICKY!

¡¡BABALÚ!!

LUCILLE BALL

DESI ARNAZ

THE EARLY 1950's ALSO MARKED THE APPEARANCE OF LATINO STARS, LIKE CUBAN "RICKY RICARDO."

IN THE 1950's, SPICY FOOD BEGAN TO APPEAR IN THE MAINSTREAM AMERICAN DIET FOR THE FIRST TIME. SALSA, BURRITOS, NACHOS, TEQUILA, TACOS...

¿QUÉ ES ESO?

THE WORD BURRITO IN SPANISH MEANS "DONKEY."

MANY OF THESE DISHES WERE TEX-MEX INVENTIONS. IN MEXICO, ONLY PEOPLE IN DURANGO KNEW WHAT A BURRITO WAS. IT WAS A LOCALS-ONLY TREAT.

CHOCOLATE WAS AN AZTEC DRINK. THE EUROPEANS BROUGHT IT BACK TO THE OLD CONTINENT AS A RESULT OF THE CONQUEST.

AVOCADO - "AGUACATE" - IS THE EQUIVALENT OF BUTTER TO THOSE WHO SPOKE NAHUATL, A PRE-COLUMBIAN TONGUE. A FAVORITE AZTEC FRUIT, AGUACATE WAS SMOOSHED AND SPREAD OUT.

I LIKE YOUR STYLE, COMPADRE!

TEXAS

BURRITO SECTION

NORTEÑA FOOD, FROM THE NORTHERN MEXICAN STATES, HAS GREATLY INFLUENCED TEX-MEX CUISINE. BARBACOA, TO NAME AN EXAMPLE, IS THE ROOT OF WHAT AMERICANS CALL ...

B-B-Q! (BARBECUE)

TACOS, OF COURSE, HAVE BEEN POPULAR IN THE SOUTHWEST FOR GENERATIONS. CHILI CON CARNE, ON THE OTHER HAND, IS AN ANGLO VERSION OF THE TRADITIONAL MEXICAN ASOPADO, A MIX OF MEAT AND SOUP THAT PROBABLY DATES BACK TO COLONIAL TIMES.

CHILI CON CARNE MEANS "CHILE WITH MEAT."

YOU KNOW, I'VE BEEN THINKING. WE'RE SURELY OFFERING A BROAD VIEW OF LATINO EVENTS IN THIS BOOK. BUT THE AUTHOR CONCENTRATES MAINLY ON NOTABLE FIGURES AND TURNING POINTS IN HISTORY. SHOULD HISTORY BE AN ACCOUNT OF THE WAY FAMOUS INDIVIDUALS LIVED AT VARIOUS PERIODS IN TIME OR ABOUT THE MASSES?

A CLEVER QUESTION... I GUESS IT DEPENDS ON WHO IS PULLING THE STRINGS.

NACHOS

HISTORY IS NOTHING BUT THE ATTEMPT TO SYSTEMATIZE HUMAN MEMORY. AND MEMORY IS SO FRAGILE, SO SUBJECTIVE. EACH HISTORIAN ENDS UP WRITING AN ACCOUNT THAT IS SUITABLE, CONVENIENT TO HIM, THAT JUSTIFIES THE PAST IN HIS EYES.

OH, THIS IS TOO MUCH... ¡OLVIDALO! FORGET ABOUT IT!

MEANWHILE IN NEW YORK...

MANHATTAN WAS A CENTER OF INTELLECTUAL AND ARTISTIC LIFE, AND MANY ASPIRING HISPANIC PAINTERS AND WRITERS CONSIDERED THE CITY A SOURCE OF INSPIRATION. THAT LADY IS **JULIA DE BURGOS**, PUERTO RICO'S MOST IMPORTANT POET. SHE WAS BORN IN **1914** IN THE ISLAND'S COUNTRYSIDE. IN NEW YORK, SHE WAS POLITICALLY ACTIVE WHILE WRITING POEMS AND <u>CANCIONES</u>.

SHE SUFFERED FROM DEPRESSION AND ALCOHOLISM. IN 1953, SHE WAS FOUND DEAD, WITH NO IDENTIFICATION, ON THE STREET. IRONICALLY, SHE HAD PREVIOUSLY WRITTEN POEMS ABOUT HER FUTURE ANONYMOUS DEATH.

IN 1957, THE BROADWAY MUSICAL **WEST SIDE STORY** OPENED, AN ADAPTATION OF SHAKESPEARE'S <u>ROMEO AND JULIET</u>. SET IN THE NEW YORK STREETS. THE MUSICAL FOCUSED ON TWO GANGS, ONE PUERTO RICAN, THE OTHER AMERICAN.

I WANT TO LIVE IN AMERICA!

BROADWAY AUDIENCES FELL IN LOVE WITH THE MUSIC AND DANCE, BUT PUERTO RICANS WERE OFFENDED, SAYING THEY WERE DEPICTED AS VENGEFUL AGGRESSIVE ADOLESCENTS.

COME ON! THE MOVIE WAS ONLY A WORK OF ART. NO HARM WAS MEANT. AREN'T WE ALL BEING TOO SENSITIVE?

AMOR SIN BARRERAS

MARIA, I JUST MET A GIRL NAMED MARIA!

AND WHY MARIA? WHY NOT ANOTHER NAME? ARE ALL LATINA GIRLS NAMED MARIA AND ALL BOYS PEDRO OR JUAN?

WEST SIDE STORY

1958, BUT IN THE CARIBBEAN...

THE DECADE ENDED WITH THE LOUD RESONANCE OF A REVOLUTION IN CUBA THAT WOULD AFFECT THE GLOBE.

HISTORY WILL ABSOLVE ME! LA HISTORIA ME ABSOLVERÁ...

FIDEL CASTRO, WHO HAD A PROMISING CAREER AS A LAWYER, OVERTHREW THE CORRUPT DICTATORSHIP OF FULGENCIO BATISTA. CASTRO HAD BEEN IMPRISONED SEVERAL TIMES FOR POLITICAL AGITATION. HE WAS FORCED INTO EXILE IN MEXICO, WHERE HE PREPARED HIS TROOPS FOR THEIR FINAL JOURNEY TO POWER.

1956: FIDEL, HIS BROTHER RAÚL CASTRO, CHÉ GUEVARA, AND OTHERS REHEARSE GUERILLA WARFARE.

THE SAME YEAR, THEY BOARD THE YACHT GRANMA TO OVERTHROW THE CUBAN CAPITALIST REGIME.

1958-1959: TRIUMPHANT ENTRY TO HAVANA WITH THE EJÉRCITO REBELDE-REBEL ARMY.

SAY CHEESE!

CASTRO FOUGHT FOR JUSTICE AND EQUALITY. HE BECAME THE SUPREME LEADER OF CUBA'S "REVOLUTIONARY NEW ERA!" HE WOULD NATIONALIZE WHOLE INDUSTRIES AND ERASE CATHOLICISM—AS MUCH AS POSSIBLE—FROM CUBAN SOCIETY. IT WASN'T UNTIL 1998, WHEN THE CUBAN ECONOMY WAS IN SHAMBLES, THAT CASTRO INVITED THE POPE TO CUBA AND SLOWLY ALLOWED SOME RELIGIOUS FREEDOM.

AMERICANS CONSIDERED THE ISLAND A HUGE CASINO AND TRAVELED THERE TO GAMBLE AND HAVE A GOOD TIME.

WHAT CASTRO WANTED WAS A NATION WITHOUT RICH AND POOR, WITHOUT ILLITERACY, AND WITH MEDICAL SERVICES FOR ALL. DURING THE BATISTA REGIME, THERE WAS A TREMENDOUS GAP BETWEEN THE UPPER AND LOWER CLASSES.

THE UNITED STATES TRIED TO STOP CASTRO BUT COULDN'T. AMERICAN LEADERS BEGAN TO FEAR THAT THE GHOST OF COMMUNISM WOULD SPREAD ALL OVER THE AMERICAS.

IN **1961** PRESIDENT **JOHN F. KENNEDY**, FURIOUS AT FIDEL CASTRO BECAUSE OF HIS IRREVERENT APPROACH TO THE U.S., BROKE OFF DIPLOMATIC RELATIONS WITH HAVANA. SHORTLY AFTERWARDS, HE ORDERED A MILITARY OPERATION. AMERICAN-BACKED CUBAN EXILES DESCENDED ON **CUBA'S BAY OF PIGS**, BUT THEIR STRATEGY BACK-FIRED AS THE CUBAN RESISTANCE TO THE WOULD-BE INVASION NEUTRALIZED THEM.

IT WAS AN EMBARRASSMENT FOR WASHINGTON.

HELLO, USA, COME IN... OVER...

I SAID HELLO?!

TALK TO THE HAND!

FIDEL

1962 THE CONSEQUENCES OF BAY OF PIGS WERE FAR REACHING. A YEAR LATER, A TENSE CRISIS BETWEEN THE SOVIET EMPIRE AND THE UNITED STATES FOCUSED ON A SET OF **MISSLES IN CUBA**

USA → THIS WAY

THAT WAS THE TIME I DECLARED MY ALLIANCE TO MOSCOW. IN RETALIATION, THE WHITE HOUSE ORCHES-TRATED AN INTERNATIONAL ECONOMIC BLOCKADE FORBIDDING WESTERN NATIONS TO DO BUSINESS WITH US.

THE ECONOMIC EMBARGO WILL BRING CASTRO DOWN!!

NO, THE EMBARGO IS GIVING HIM STAMINA TO REMAIN IN POWER.

HELMS

U.S. SENATE

MÁS VALE MORIR PARADO QUE VIVIR DE RODILLAS.

THE MIDDLE-AND-UPPER-CLASS IN CUBA DECIDED TO SEEK EXILE.

A ROUGH TRANSLATION, BETTER TO LIVE ELSE WHERE THAN TO LIVE HERE DISPOSSESSED!

AROUND 1,000,000 CUBANS EMIGRATED. MANY WENT TO SPAIN AND LATIN AMERICA, BUT THE MAJORITY FLED TO THE UNITED STATES, AND SETTLED IN FLORIDA. THEY ARRIVED AS POLITICAL REFUGEES, A "STATUS THAT PROVIDED THEM WITH GOVERNMENT BENEFITS.

IT WAS AMONG CUBAN REFUGEES IN DADE COUNTY, FLORIDA, THAT **BILINGUAL EDUCATION** BEGAN IN IN 1960.

abc

YO ME LLAMO MARIA

YO ME LLAMO MARIA.

¿Y TÚ?

¿Y TÚ?

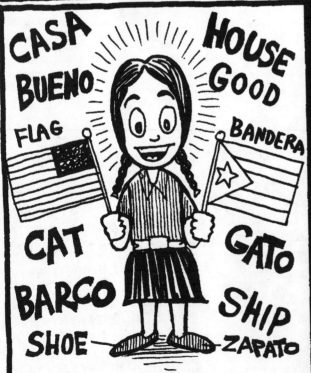

CASA

HOUSE

BUENO

GOOD

FLAG

BANDERA

CAT

GATO

BARCO

SHIP

SHOE

ZAPATO

BILINGUAL EDUCATION WAS DESIGNED TO HELP RECENT CUBAN EXILES REMAIN LOYAL TO THE MOTHER TONGUE, SPANISH. MANY THOUGHT CASTRO'S REGIME WOULD ONLY LAST A FEW MONTHS, PERHAPS A COUPLE OF YEARS. THEY WANTED THEIR CHILDREN TO CONTINUE THEIR EDUCATION WHILE THEY WAITED TO RETURN TO CUBA.

MEANWHILE IN LITTLE HAVANA...

LA ROSITA Restaurante

CAFE

¡HOLA CHICO!

¡VAYA!

THE WAIT, OF COURSE, STRETCHED INTO A DECADE, AND THEN TWO, THREE... AND BILINGUAL EDUCATION WAS SOON ESTABLISHED AS A PROGRAM TO HELP IMMIGRANT STUDENTS ACQUIRE FLUENCY IN ENGLISH WITHOUT LOSING SCHOOL TIME.

THE GOVERNMENT PAYS FOR SPANISH TEACHERS, AND ALLOWS SPANISH TO BECOME A LEGITIMATE LANGUAGE IN THE SCHOOLS!

GOP

ENGLISH IS OUR COUNTRY'S "GREAT EQUALIZER." IT IS THE SOLE OFFICIAL LANGUAGE OF THE UNITED STATES. WE SHOULD NOT TEACH OUR CHILDREN ANY OTHER TONGUE IN PUBLIC SCHOOLS.

HE'S WRONG! ONLY IN AMERICA CAN YOU BE PENALIZED FOR BEING BILINGUAL. IN MOST OTHER COUNTRIES IT IS CONSIDERED BETTER, EVEN AN ASSET, TO KNOW TWO LANGUAGES.

BUT OF COURSE. WHAT FOOLISHNESS!

US SENATE

NO LOITERING

TODAY, DECADES AFTER BILINGUAL EDUCATION WAS ESTABLISHED, IT REMAINS CONTROVERSIAL. MEANWHILE, SPANISH IS SPOKEN THROUGHOUT THE U.S.

EL SHOW DE CRISTINA

107

AFTER WORLD WAR II, PUERTO RICO'S ECONOMY WAS IN SHAMBLES. AFTER THE WAR, THE PUERTO RICAN GOVERNMENT GAVE TAX INCENTIVES TO FOREIGN AND LOCAL INVESTORS, BUT THE EFFECT ON THE RURAL POPULATION WAS MINIMAL. BEGINNING IN THE 1940'S, AS A RESULT OF THE JONES ACT, SIGNED IN 1917 BY PRESIDENT WOODROW WILSON, A MASSIVE IMMIGRATION OF JÍBAROS FROM PUERTO RICO'S COUNTRYSIDE DESCENDED ON NEW YORK.

RACE AND RICHES ESCALATED HOSTILE RELATIONS AMONG LATINOS. CUBAN EXILES WERE WHITE AND MIDDLE CLASS, WHEREAS PUERTO RICAN JÍBAROS THAT ARRIVED IN THE 50's AND 60's WERE POOR AND BLACK OR MIXED RACE.

THE ASSASINATION OF **PRESIDENT JOHN KENNEDY** SENT WAVES OF FEAR THROUGHOUT THE U.S. SOME BELIEVED THE FATAL BULLET WAS FIRED BY FIDEL CASTRO'S SUPPORTERS.

(STONE)

108

THE STRUGGLE AMONG BLACKS TO END SEGREGATION - A LEGACY OF SLAVERY - BROUGHT ABOUT THE CIVIL RIGHTS MOVEMENT, A SERIES OF POLITICAL EVENTS SEEKING A FAIRER, MORE INTEGRATED SOCIETY. THE MOST PROMINENT FIGURE CENTRAL TO THIS EFFORT WAS **REVEREND MARTIN LUTHER KING, JR.**

AMONG LATINOS, A SIMILAR STRUGGLE AGAINST RACISM AND INJUSTICE GAINED MOMENTUM. IT CAME TO BE KNOWN AS **EL MOVIMIENTO.**

REIES LÓPEZ TIJERINA WAS THE LEADER OF THE **ALIANZA FEDERAL DE MERCEDES**, A GROUP PROTESTING VIOLATIONS OF CIVIL RIGHTS AND LAND POSSESSION. IN 1967, MEMBERS OF THE GROUP TOOK CONTROL OF A COURTHOUSE IN **TIERRA AMARILLA, NEW MEXICO.** IN RETALIATION, U.S. TROOPS DESCENDED UPON THE WHOLE REGION IN AN ATTEMPT TO RESTORE ORDER.

TIERRA Ó MUERTE!

ALSO IN 1967, PUERTO RICANS VOTED TO REMAIN A COMMONWEALTH AND THUS REJECTED INDEPENDENCE.

THE SIXTIES

WERE YEARS OF REVOLUTION. THE HIPPIE GENERATION LOOKED INWARD, FIGHTING AGAINST THE "ESTABLISHMENT." BUDDHISM AND OTHER ASIAN RELIGIONS AND PHILOSOPHIES BECAME A MAGNET FOR THE YOUNG IN THE WESTERN HEMISPHERE. BOOKS LIKE **CARLOS CASTANEDA'S THE TEACHINGS OF DON JUAN,** AN ANTHROPOLOGICAL STUDY OF MAGIC AND SHAMANISM AMONG THE MEXICAN INDIANS OF OAXACA, PUBLISHED IN 1968, CAPTIVATED THE WORLD. IN 1965, UNITED STATES INVOLVEMENT IN THE NEEDLESS **VIETNAM WAR,** ATTEMPTED TO STOP THE SPREAD OF **COMMUNISM** IN SOUTHEAST ASIA. ATTEMPTS TO DEMOCRATIZE SOME EASTERN EUROPEAN NATIONS WERE MET WITH MILITARY INTERVENTION BY THE SOVIET UNION. A SERIES OF STUDENT UPRISINGS AT THE **UNIVERSITY OF CALIFORNIA AT BERKELEY** AND **COLUMBIA UNIVERSITY,** AS WELL AS IN PARIS, OFTEN ENDED IN BLOODY CONFRONTATIONS WITH THE POLICE.

CASTRO'S CUBA BECAME A MODEL OF REBELLION.

PRAGUE SPRING, 1968

STUDENT PROTESTORS WERE MASSACRED IN MEXICO CITY'S TLATELOLCO SQUARE, 1968

THROUGHOUT **THE SOUTHWEST**, CHICANOS BEGAN TO MOBILIZE IN PROTEST AGAINST THE POOR CONDITIONS OF MIGRANT WORKERS IN COTTON AND GRAPE FIELDS. STUDENTS AND DOMESTIC WORKERS ALSO JOINED THE CAUSE.

OTHER LEADERS SUCH AS RODOLFO "CORKY" GONZALES JOINED TIJERINA IN A "CRUSADE FOR JUSTICE!"

"CORKY" GONZÁLEZ WAS A FEATHERWEIGHT BOXING CHAMP IN THE 1950's, BUT LATER BECAME A POLITICAL ACTIVIST. HE WAS ALSO A BUSINESSMAN AND HELPED FOUND LOS VOLUNTARIOS, AN ORGANIZATION THAT WAS INSTRUMENT-AL IN DEVELOPING EL PLAN ESPIRITUAL DE AZTLÁN, A PROGRAM TO REVITAL-IZE THE POLITICAL AND CULTURAL SOUL OF THE PEOPLE OF AZTLÁN.

YES, "CORKY" WAS A SPIRITUAL LEADER. HE WAS A POET WHOSE LEGACY CAN BE FOUND IN THE POLITICAL MAN-IFESTO, YO SOY JOAQUÍN.

Here I stand
    before the Court of Justice
        Guilty
for all the glory of my Raza
    to be sentenced to despair.
Here I stand
    Poor In Money
    Arrogant with pride
    Bold with Machismo
    Rich in courage
            and
    Wealthy in spirit and faith
My knees are caked with mud.
My hands, callused from the hoe.
I have made the Anglo rich
            yet
    Equality is but a word,
        the Treaty of
        Guadalupe Hidalgo has been
        broken
        and is but another
        treacherous promise.
My land is lost
    and stolen,
My culture has been raped,
        I lengthen
    the line at the welfare door.

IN THE MANIFESTO, "CORKY" BECOMES THE QUINTESSENTIAL CHICANO SPIRIT, THE POETIC VOICE OF THE STRUGGLE — EL ALMA EN VOZ. HE NAVIGATES THROUGH TIME AND SPACE TO BE EVERYWHERE AND BECOME EVERYONE.

A SENSE OF EMPOWER-MENT TOOK OVER. THE MYTH OF AZTLÁN WAS IN EVERYONES MIND. THE UNITED STATES WAS AT WAR WITH ITSELF. INTERNAL COLONIALISM WAS EVIL. CHICANOS ARGUED FOR LIBERATION, FOR A RETURN TO THEIR HOMELAND: AZTLÁN.

IN 1968, SENATOR ROBERT F. KENNEDY, BROTHER OF SLAIN PRESIDENT KENNEDY AND A CLOSE FRIEND OF CÉSAR CHÁVEZ, WAS ASSASSINATED IN LOS ANGELES. THE FOLLOWING YEAR, THERE WAS AN ATTEMPT TO CREATE A CHICANO POLITICAL PARTY THAT WOULD CHALLENGE THE TWO-PARTY SYSTEM.

LA RAZA UNIDA PARTY

LA RAZA UNIDA PARTY

TEXAS

CHICANO POWER

CALIFAS

VIVA LA RAZA UNIDA PARTY

LA RAZA UNIDA

LRU PARTY

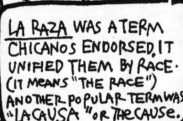

LA RAZA WAS A TERM CHICANOS ENDORSED, IT UNIFIED THEM BY RACE. (IT MEANS "THE RACE") ANOTHER POPULAR TERM WAS "LA CAUSA" OR THE CAUSE.

LA RAZA UNIDA PARTY CAME ABOUT AT THE NATIONAL CHICANO YOUTH LIBERATION CONFERENCE IN DENVER, COLORADO. THE **GRINGO** WAS ITS ENEMY.

CONFERENCIA

THE ANIMOSITY THAT MARKED THOSE YEARS REFLECTED A LONG HISTORY OF OPPRESSION. CHICANOS WERE READY TO SEIZE THEIR DESTINY. THE PARTY HAD AS ITS GOALS:

1. The creation of voter registration programs that would help increase participation of Chicanos at the polls.
2. The search for ways to connect politicians with the working people.
3. A more equal distribution of wealth.
4. The more active role of women in society, one equal to men.
5. The abolition of the Texas Rangers.
6. The reduction of taxes to working people.
7. The passing of legislation to largely improve the status of "illegal aliens" in U.S. territory and to provide them with education and services.

LA RAZA UNIDA PARTY MUST BECOME MORE THAN A POLITICAL ORGANIZATION. IT MUST SYMBOLIZE THE CREATION OF A NATION WITHIN A NATION, A SPIRITUAL UNIFICATION FOR EFFECTIVE ACTION OF ALL PERSONS OF MEXICAN DESCENT IN THE UNITED STATES. ONE PRINCIPLE DOMINATES LA RAZA UNIDA THOUGHT— THAT THE DESTINY OF EACH CHICANO IS IMMUTABLY LINKED TO THE DESTINY OF EVERY OTHER CHICANO.

ACCORDING TO THE **1960 CENSUS**, THERE WERE ALMOST **4,000,000 CHICANOS** IN THE U.S. THEY WERE THE SECOND LARGEST MINORITY GROUP IN THE COUNTRY.

THIS GRAPH COURTESY OF TOTALLY UNSCIENTIFIC GRAPHS, INC.

IN **1965**, PRESIDENT JOHNSON SIGNED THE **VOTING RIGHTS ACT** ELIMINATING ALL DISCRIMINATORY QUALIFYING TESTS FOR VOTER REGISTRATION.

THE SAME YEAR, **CÉSAR CHÁVEZ** BEGAN ORGANIZING HIS FELLOW FARM WORKERS, NOT ONLY CHICANOS BUT ALSO FILIPINOS.

HE WAS NOT THE FIRST TO ATTEMPT A _HUELGA_ AMONG THE FARM WORKERS. BUT FEW HAD SUCCEEDED BEFORE HIM. SINCE MIGRANT WORKERS ARE ALWAYS ON THE MOVE, IT WAS DIFFICULT TO BRING THEM TO SUPPORT A LABOR OBJECTIVE.

HUELGA

THE MOST FAMOUS OF ALL CHICANO ACTIVISTS THE ONE WHO ACHIEVED NOT ONLY NATIONAL BUT GLOBAL RECOGNITION, WAS **CÉSAR CHÁVEZ.** HIS PHILOSOPHY WAS INSPIRED EQUALLY BY MAHATMA GANDHI'S PACIFISM AND BY THE REV. MARTIN LUTHER KING, JR'S NONVIOLENT RESISTANCE.

HE WAS BORN IN **1927** IN **YUMA, ARIZONA.** HIS FATHER OWNED A 160-ACRE FARM, BUT LOST IT DURING THE DEPRESSION. THIS INCIDENT PUSHED THE FAMILY TO POVERTY. THEY WERE FORCED TO BECOME MIGRANT WORKERS, PICKING CARROTS, COTTON, AND OTHER PRODUCE.

HE DIDN'T FINISH HIGH SCHOOL!

TIME TO MOVE, CÉSAR!

HE LIVED AS A FARM WORKER, MIGRATING FROM TOWN TO TOWN, ACCORDING TO THE CROP SEASONS. CÉSAR ATTENDED **37 SCHOOLS!**

TIME

CESAR CHAVEZ

In **1967**, CHÁVEZ BECAME THE FIRST CHICANO TO APPEAR ON THE COVER OF **TIME** MAGAZINE. HE WAS PORTRAYED AS THE "MEXICAN-AMERICAN DR. MARTIN LUTHER KING, JR."

ABOUT TIME

¡VENCEREMOS!

¡FUERA DE VIETNAM!

A MILITANT GENERATION.

VIVA LA RAZA

A YOUNG GENERATION OF CHICANOS WAS ENTHUSIASTIC TO JOIN THE FIGHT FOR SOCIAL JUSTICE. STUDENTS ON CAMPUSES ACROSS THE SOUTHWEST BEGAN TO MARCH IN SUPPORT OF CHÁVEZ AND THE UNITED FARM WORKERS. JOURNALS LIKE **EL GRITO** AND **CON SAFOS** WERE PUBLISHED, AND SPEECHES WERE DELIVERED.

CHÁVEZ WAS VERY EFFECTIVE. IN THE NEXT FIVE YEARS, HIS MOVEMENT GAINED INTERNATIONAL FOLLOWERS. HIS STRATEGY WAS TO FORCE GRAPE FIELD OWNERS TO CHANGE, BUT NOT THROUGH CONFRONTATION. HE WAS A PACIFIST.

I WILL NOT EAT AGAIN UNTIL THE GRAPE GROWERS CONCEDE...

HE JOINED FORCES WITH **REIES LÓPEZ TIJERINA** AND OTHER LEADERS AND ORGANIZED A BOYCOTT AGAINST GRAPE GROWERS.

THE WHOLE ERA IS KNOWN AS THE **CHICANO MOVEMENT.** THEATER TROUPES, LIKE **EL TEATRO CAMPESINO,** LED BY DIRECTOR **LUIS VALDEZ,** WERE FORMED TO RAISE THE POLITICAL AND CULTURAL CONSCIOUSNESS OF CHICANOS.

PÁJARO

PATRÓN

TRABAJADOR

LUIS VALDEZ WOULD LATER BECOME A FAMOUS HOLLYWOOD DIRECTOR. AMONG HIS MOVIES ARE **LA BAMBA,** ABOUT THE LEGENDARY CHICANO ROCK-AND-ROLLER **RITCHIE VALENS,** WHO DIED IN A PLANE CRASH IN 1959, ALONG WITH BUDDY HOLLY AND "THE BIG BOPPER."

LOS LOBOS

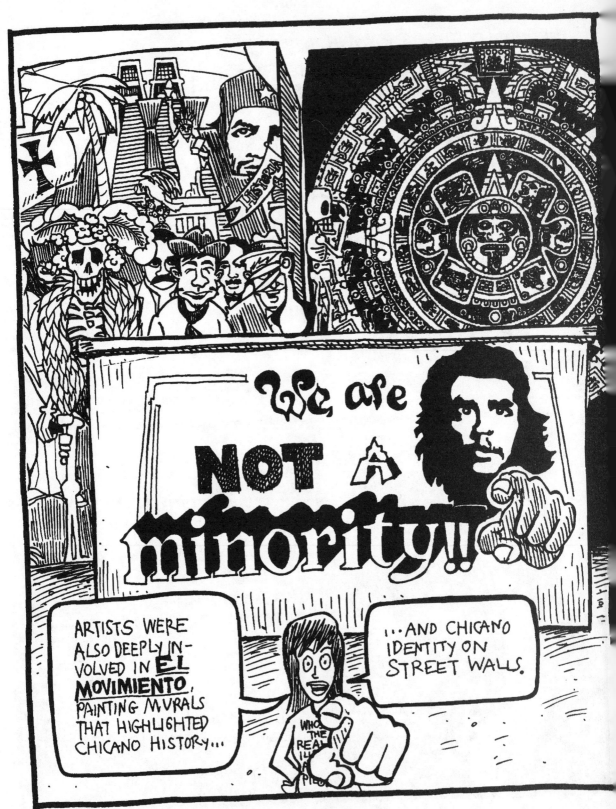

ARTISTS WERE ALSO DEEPLY INVOLVED IN **EL MOVIMIENTO**, PAINTING MURALS THAT HIGHLIGHTED CHICANO HISTORY...

...AND CHICANO IDENTITY ON STREET WALLS.

A PARAMILITARY GROUP, KNOWN AS THE **BROWN BERETS**, WAS FORMED BY ACTIVIST STUDENTS. MODELED AFTER THE BLACK PANTHERS, THEY WERE FORMED IN EAST LOS ANGELES IN 1967 AS A GROUP CALLED **YOUNG CITIZENS FOR COMMUNITY ACTION**.

BROWN

NOT ONLY CHICANOS ARE UP IN ARMS! SO ARE WE, THE PUERTO RICAN PEOPLE. RACISM AND INJUSTICE ARE EVERY WHERE...

PURPLE

YOUNG LORDS

ON THE EAST COAST, THE **PUERTO RICAN YOUNG LORDS** ORGANIZED THEMSELVES AS WELL. THEY WERE REVOLUTIONARY NATIONALISTS BATTLING THE UNITED STATES FOR ITS ILL TREATMENT OF THE PUERTO RICAN COMMUNITY AND FOR KEEPING PUERTO RICO AS A COLONY, NOT ALLOWING IT ITS INDEPENDENCE.

BORICUA POWER

ABAJO CON EL USA

NYPD

THE U.S. GOVERNMENT, MARRED BY CORRUPTION AND SCANDAL, WAS PERCEIVED AS UNCOMMITTED TO PUERTO RICANS IN PARTICULAR AND LATINOS IN GENERAL.

AMONG THE MOST RADICAL AND INTERESTING POLITICAL FIGURES OF THE TIME WAS CHICANO **OSCAR "ZETA" ACOSTA**, A LAWYER AND WRITER. HE IS THE FAMOUS SAMOAN ATTORNEY IN HUNTER S. THOMPSON'S CLASSIC **FEAR AND LOATHING IN LAS VEGAS.** "ZETA" WAS A DRUG ADDICT AND PROBABLY A DRUG TRAFFICKER TOO. HIS FRIENDSHIP WITH THOMPSON, THE FAMOUS "GONZO JOURNALIST" WAS, TO SOME EXTENT, A DOOR TO "ZETA" FOR BOOK CONTRACTS AND HIGH PROFILE POLITICS.

LA MUNICIPAL COURT

I OBJECT TO THE GRINGO'S LAW!

ALTHOUGH I WAS BORN IN EL PASO, TEXAS, I AM ACTUALLY A SMALL-TOWN KID. A HICK FROM THE STICKS, A MEXICAN BOY FROM THE OTHER SIDE OF THE TRACKS.

LAS VEGAS

THE AUTOBIOGRAPHY OF A **BROWN BUFFALO**

"**REVOLT OF THE COCKROACH PEOPLE**"

ZETA PROBABLY TOOK HIS NAME FROM THE FAMOUS "**ZORRO**." HE SAW HIMSELF AS A ROBIN HOOD OF SORTS, ACTIVELY DEFENDING CHICANOS IN CALIFORNIA COURTROOMS. HE RAN FOR SHERIFF OF LOS ANGELES COUNTY, WROTE A COUPLE OF BOOKS, AND DISAPPEARED MYSTERIOUSLY IN MAZATLÁN, MEXICO, IN **1974**.

FROM A CARTOON BY SERGIO HERNANDEZ IN CON SAFOS MAGAZINE c/s

IN **1971**, BLACK REVOLUTIONARY GEORGE JACKSON WAS KILLED WHILE TRYING TO ESCAPE SAN QUENTIN PRISON. SIX PRISONERS — BLACKS AND LATINOS — WERE ACCUSED, AMONG THEM LUIS TALAMANTEZ.

I DEFENDED LUIS TALAMANTEZ, ONE OF THE SAN QUENTIN SIX!

NO YOU DIDN'T! YOU ABANDONED THE CASE!

(LUIS TALAMANTEZ) →

ACOSTA FOR SHERIFF

SHAMELESS PLUG! ←

BANDINO BY LAU

127

DEMOCRÁCIA EN LATINO AMERICA

MEANWHILE, DEMOCRACY IN LATIN AMERICA CONTINUED TO BE ELUSIVE.

PELIGRO ELECTRICO

DEATH TO THE COMMUNISTS! I CAN ARRANGE IT...

SALVADOR ALLENDE

PINOCHET

MILITARY DICTATORSHIPS, OFTEN BACKED BY THE UNITED STATES, WERE THE ONLY RESPONSE TO ATTEMPTS AT ESTABLISHING A FREER, MORE PLURALISTIC SOCIETY. IN 1973, LEFT-WING PRESIDENT SALVADOR ALLENDE WON NATIONAL ELECTIONS IN CHILE. BUT HIS TENURE WAS SHORT- ARMY STRONGMAN AUGUSTO PINOCHET ORCHESTRATED A COUP D'ETAT IN WHICH ALLENDE NOT ONLY FELL FROM POWER, BUT ALSO COMMITTED "SUICIDE."

DICTATOR-SHIP FOR DUMMIES!

MANUAL DEL PERFECTO IDIOTA LATINO-AMERICANO

128

EL AUTOR IN IL POSTINO

THE LEGENDARY CHILEAN POET **PABLO NERUDA**, WHO WAS AWARDED THE NOBEL PRIZE FOR LITERATURE, FELT VERY CLOSE TO CHICANOS AND PUERTO RICANS IN THE UNITED STATES. AMONG HIS WORKS ARE A PLAY ABOUT JOAQUÍN MURRIETA, AS WELL AS POEMS TO THE MARTYRS OF <u>EL MOVIMIENTO</u>. ONE OF HIS POEMS HONORS **JUAN DE LA CRUZ**, A 60-YEAR OLD <u>CAMPESINO</u> KILLED IN 1973 DURING A STRIKE OF THE UNITED FARM WORKERS UNION.

NERUDA IS AN ADMIRED FIGURE AMONG MILITANT LATINOS, ALTHOUGH HE WAS EXILED FROM THE U.S. BECAUSE OF HIS COMMUNIST IDEAS.

Behind the liberation
was Juan
working, fishing and
struggling
in his carpentry or in his
damp mine.
His hands have worked the
land and measured
the roads.
His bones are everywhere.
But he lives. He returned from the land.
He is born.
He has been born again like an eternal
plant.
All the night's impurity tried to bury him
and now, in the dawn, he speaks with lips
that will not be sealed.

129

AMONG THE MARTYRS OF EL MOVIMIENTO WAS **RUBÉN SALAZAR** A DISTINGUISHED JOURNALIST EMPLOYED AS NEWS DIRECTOR OF **KMEX**, THE SPANISH-LANGUAGE TELEVISION IN LOS ANGELES. HE STARTED A WEEKLY COLUMN FOR THE **LOS ANGELES TIMES** ON CHICANO ISSUES. HE WAS NEVER AFRAID TO BE VOCAL ABOUT THE BRUTALITY AND ABUSE THE LA POLICE INFLICTED ON CHICANOS.

COMMENTARY by RUBÉN SALAZAR

"Who is a Chicano? And what is it the Chicanos want? A Chicano is a Mexican-American with a non-Anglo image of himself. He resents being told Columbus "discovered" America when the Chicano's ancestors, the Mayans and the Aztecs, founded highly sophisticated civilizations centuries before Spain financed the Italian explorer's trip to the "New World." Chicanos also resent Anglo pronouncements that Chicanos are "culturally deprived" or that the fact that they speak Spanish is a "problem.""

NATIONAL CHICANO MORATORIUM, L.A., 1970

IN 1970, SOME 30,000 PEOPLE MARCHED IN THE STREETS OF LOS ANGELES, RESISTING THE **VIETNAM WAR** AND ACCUSING THE GOVERNMENT OF INTERNAL RACISM. CHICANOS WERE BEING DRAFTED IN OUTRAGEOUS PROPORTIONS.

THAT DAY—**AUGUST 29**—THE POLICE INTERVENED AND A RIOT ERUPTED. **RUBÉN SALAZAR** WAS KILLED BY A STRAY GAS CANISTER IN THE SILVER DOLLAR CAFÉ. SALAZAR AND THE MORATORIUM WERE FOREVER MEMORIALIZED.

SOON AFTER, AN ALLIANCE WAS ESTABLISHED AMONG ALL THE HAVE-NOTS: PUERTO RICANS, CHICANOS, BLACKS AND NATIVE-AMERICANS

THE SIXTIES WERE FULL OF CHANGE—AND THEY ALSO BROUGHT AN EXTRAORDINARY ARRAY OF LITERARY TALENTS FROM LATIN AMERICA. THESE WRITERS—ESPECIALLY **GABRIEL GARCIA MÁRQUEZ,** WITH HIS MASTERPIECE <u>ONE HUNDRED YEARS OF SOLITUDE</u>—REINTRODUCED THE SPANISH-SPEAKING WORLD TO AN INTERNATIONAL READERSHIP BY STRESSING THE LINK BETWEEN DREAMS AND REALITY, BETWEEN MAGIC AND SCIENCE, BETWEEN THE EUROPEAN INFLUENCE IN LIFE AND THE PRE-COLUMBIAN CIVILIZATIONS.

TRUE... PEOPLE THE WORLD OVER WERE FOCUSING THEIR ATTENTION ON THE SOUTHERN HEMISPHERE. BUT HISPANICS IN THE UNITED STATES DIDN'T BENEFIT FROM THE INTEREST! EVEN THOUGH CHÁVEZ AND HIS SUPPORTERS WERE MUCH ADMIRED, LATINOS WERE GENERALLY PERCEIVED AS DANGEROUS—A THREAT TO SOCIETY.

BLESS ME ULTIMA

IN THE EARLY 1970's, AT THE TIME OF THE CIVIL RIGHTS UPHEAVAL, A NUMBER OF WRITERS, AMONG THEM **TOMÁS RIVERA** AND **RUDOLFO ANAYA**, WROTE NOVELS ABOUT MIGRANT WORKERS AND **CURANDERAS**, NATURAL HEALERS IN THE SOUTHWEST. THESE NOVELS WOULD BECOME CLASSICS. THE LITERARY FIESTA WAS ALSO HAPPENING, ALBEIT ON A SMALLER SCALE, NORTH OF THE RIO GRANDE

THE SEVENTIES WERE YEARS OF RECESSION.

MECHA

THE ENORMOUS EXPANSION OF FREE SPIRITED ENERGY WAS FOLLOWED BY A SLOWDOWN. PEOPLE MOVED AWAY FROM RADICALISM, ENDORSING A MORE CONSERVATIVE VIEW OF LIFE. THE U.S. WAS FORCED TO END THE VIETNAM WAR IN AN EMBARRASSING DEFEAT. WITH IT THE HIPPIE GENERATION DISCOVERED IT HAD LOST ITS <u>RAISON D'ETRE</u> - ITS REAL CAUSE.

137

138

IN 1978, WHEN PRESIDENT JIMMY CARTER WAS IN THE WHITE HOUSE, THE U.S. VOTED TO RETURN THE PANAMA CANAL TO THE PANAMANIANS IN 2000.

CARIBBEAN SEA

PANAMA CANAL

N

BAY OF PANAMA

THIS MADE PEOPLE FEEL AS IF THE AGE OF UPHEAVAL WAS OVER, REPLACED BY ONE CHARACTERIZED BY RESTRAINT.

THE PANAMA CANAL, AN ARTIFICIAL WATERWAY, IS STRATEGIC BECAUSE IT ALLOWS SHIPS TO GO FROM ONE OCEAN TO THE OTHER WITH-OUT HAVING TO REACH TIERRA DEL FUEGO.

THE CANAL WAS BUILT IN 1914. FRANCE BEGAN THE PROJECT BUT THE U.S. COMPLETED IT UNDER PRESIDENT WOODROW WILSON. THE U.S. GAINED JURISDICTION IN 1903 WHEN THE HAY·BUNAU-VARILLA TREATY WAS SIGNED. JIMMY CARTER AND PANAMANIAN RULER OMAR TORRIJOS RENEGOTIATED IT.

CHICANO HISTORY + (LATIN AMERICAN HISTORY)

AS A RESULT OF THE UPHEAVAL, SEVERAL UNIVERSITIES IN THE SOUTHWEST OPENED CHICANO STUDIES PROGRAMS, AND TEXT BOOKS BEGAN INCLUDING SOME LATIN AMERICAN HISTORY.

NOT MUCH, THOUGH...

BY 1980, CUBA CEASED TO BE A MODEL THAT OTHER LATIN AMERICAN COUNTRIES WANTED TO EMULATE. **FIDEL CASTRO** BECAME INFAMOUS FOR HIS INTOLERANCE OF OPPOSING POLITICAL VIEWS AND FOR HIS HATRED OF HOMOSEXUALS.

CUBA

DON'T FEED THE DISSIDENTS

THAT YEAR THE **PERUVIAN EMBASSY** IN HAVANA WAS TAKEN OVER BY AN OVERFLOW OF POLITICAL REFUGEES DISILLUSIONED WITH UNFULFILLED COMMUNIST PROMISES OF A BETTER FUTURE. THEY WERE READY TO LEAVE CUBA AS SOON AS THE GOVERNMENT WOULD ALLOW.

EMBAJADA DE PERU

MIAMI

142

IF YOU'RE NOT IN HERE ALREADY, YOU'RE PROBABLY NOT QUALIFIED!

CORPORATE AMERICA INC.

HIGHER EDUCATION

GOOD OL' BOYS NETWORK ZONE MINORITIES WILL BE TOWED AWAY

JOBS! JOBS SCHOOL

MEANWHILE, INTERNALLY IN THE MAINLAND U.S., THE CIVIL RIGHTS MOVEMENT PUSHED FOR PROGRAMS THAT WOULD HEAL THE RIFT OF RACIAL TENSION. THE MOST POLEMICAL OF ALL WAS **AFFIRMATIVE ACTION.**

THANKS TO AFFIRMATIVE ACTION, PEOPLE OF COLOR AND OTHER MINORITIES WERE ALLOWED MORE REPRESENTATION IN THE JOB MARKET AND IN SCHOOLS AND ACADEMIC INSTITUTIONS.

THIS MEANS THAT BY LAW, EMPLOYERS AND ADMINISTRATORS HAD TO MAKE ROOM FOR **NON-WHITES.**

COLLEGE APPLICATION

JOB APPLICATION

Hunger of Memory

AFFIRMATIVE ACTION QUALIFIES PEOPLE BY THE COLOR OF THEIR SKIN, NOT BY THEIR TALENTS AND COMPETENCE.

WRONG! IF PEOPLE WERE REALLY NOT QUALIFIED, THEY WOULD NOT GET ACCEPTED.

AFFIRMATIVE ACTION OPENED MANY DOORS, BUT NOT EVERY LATINO SUPPORTED IT...

RICHARD RODRIGUEZ, A CHILD OF MEXICANS RAISED IN SACRAMENTO, CALIFORNIA, WROTE THE BOOK **HUNGER OF MEMORY**, IN WHICH HE ATTACKED AFFIRMATIVE ACTION.

WASN'T THAT BOOK IN OUR AUTHORS LIBRARY?

YES. HE ADMIRES IT A LOT.

THE PROSE IS SUPERB — RHYTHMIC, PERSUASIVE...

SO IS RODRIGUEZ A CONSERVATIVE?

YES, BUT HIS ARGUMENT MAKES US SEE THE OTHER SIDE OF THE COIN.

AAK

ABSENCE OF MEMORY

MERCADO SAN ANTONIO

TIENDA
SE HABLA INGLES

¿PARA QUÉ APRENDER INGLÉS?

IF WE DON'T LEARN ENGLISH, THE POOR GRINGOS WILL GET LONELY...

STILL, BILINGUAL EDUCATION PROGRAMS SPREAD THROUGHOUT THE UNITED STATES, INCREASING THE POPULARITY OF SPANISH AND MAKING IT THE COUNTRY'S UNOFFICIAL SECOND LANGUAGE.

SE FIA MAÑANA.

SPANISH COULD BE HEARD NOT ONLY ON THE STREET AND IN THE CLASSROOM BUT ON TELEVISION ALL THE TIME. TWO FULL-FLEDGED TV NETWORKS, **UNIVISION** AND **TELEMUNDO** CAPITALIZED ON THE INCREASING POWER OF LATINOS.

145

A BACKLASH WAS INEVITABLE, OF COURSE, ESPECIALLY UNDER PRESIDENT RONALD REAGAN, A CONSERVATIVE. THE ENGLISH ONLY MOVEMENT STARTED IN TEXAS AS A COUNTER-ATTACK ON THE THREATENING INFLUENCE OF SPANISH AND OTHER IMMIGRANT LANGUAGES. THE LEGEND GOES THAT AN OLD LADY ENTERED A POST OFFICE IN HOUSTON, TEXAS AND FOUND NOT A SINGLE ENGLISH SPEAKING CLERK.

... AND THE OUTCOME WAS A XENOPHOBIC BACKLASH.

AT THE SAME TIME, **CIVIL UNREST IN CENTRAL AMERICA** BROUGHT COUNTLESS POLITICAL REFUGEES AND ILLEGAL IMMIGRANTS UP NORTH, INFUSING THE LATINO COMMUNITY WITH NEW BLOOD.

AT ONE POINT, ONE OUT OF TWO SALVADORANS LIVED IN THE UNITED STATES — IN FLORIDA, TEXAS AND THE NORTHEAST.

I LEFT BECAUSE OF THE VIOLENCE! AND SOME **2,500,000** OF MY COMPATRIOTS DID TOO.

¡BÚM! PÚM PÚM

EL SALVADOR

ANOTHER KEY PLAYER IN THE LATINO CHESS-BOARD IS THE **DOMINICAN REPUBLIC.** ITS TROUBLED HISTORY IS FILLED WITH TYRANNICAL, CORRUPT POLITICIANS, AND A MILITARY OCCUPATION BY THE UNITED STATES THAT LASTED FROM 1916 TO 1924.

D.R.

THE LONGEST DICTATORSHIP OF THE TWENTIETH CENTURY IS THAT OF **RAFAEL LEÓNIDAS TRUJILLO,** WHO RULED THE DOMINICAN REPUBLIC FROM 1930 TO 1961. HE INITIATED PROGRAMS TO PROMOTE AGRICULTURE AND PUBLIC WORKS, AND STRUGGLED TO MAKE THE DOMINICAN REPUBLIC A MODERN NATION. IN SPITE OF THE INTENSE REPRESSION, THE ECONOMY GREW TREMENDOUSLY.

148

MINERVA, PATRIA, AND MARÍA TERESA MIRABAL, THE WIVES OF PROMINENT OPPOSITION MEN, AND THEIR DRIVER, RUFINO DE LA CRUZ, WERE FOUND DEAD ON NOVEMBER 25 NEAR THEIR WRECKED JEEP AT THE BOTTOM OF A CLIFF. THIS WAS OBVIOUSLY THE JOB OF TRUJILLO'S SECRET SERVICES, LOOKING TO "SILENCE" THE WOMEN'S VOCAL OPPOSITION TO THE GOVERNMENT. THEIR DEATHS GENERATED DEEP RESENTMENT AGAINST EL DICTADOR.

NYC

WHEN TRUJILLO WAS ASSASSINATED IN 1961 THE DOMINICAN ECONOMY SUFFERED TREMENDOUSLY. PEOPLE LOST THEIR JOBS AND MANY IMMIGRATED TO THE U.S.

THEY BROUGHT ALONG MERENGUES, PLENAS, AND OTHER NATIONAL RHYTHMS AS WELL AS THEIR OWN CUISINE AND JOIE DE VIVRE.

YO NO SOY BORICUA SINO DOMINICANO

¡AL SON DEL MERENGUE!

149

THE EIGHTIES SHOULD BE CALLED "THE DECADE OF PAN-ETHNIC RELATIONS." FOR THE FIRST TIME IN HISTORY, LATINOS OF DIFFERENT BACKGROUNDS BEGAN TO FEEL THEY WERE PART OF ONE AND THE SAME MINORITY GROUP.

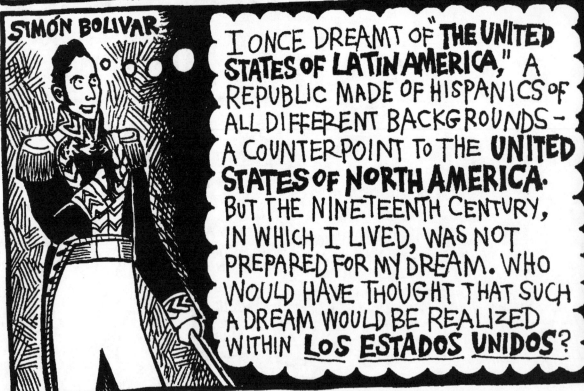

SIMÓN BOLÍVAR

I ONCE DREAMT OF "THE UNITED STATES OF LATIN AMERICA," A REPUBLIC MADE OF HISPANICS OF ALL DIFFERENT BACKGROUNDS — A COUNTERPOINT TO THE UNITED STATES OF NORTH AMERICA. BUT THE NINETEENTH CENTURY, IN WHICH I LIVED, WAS NOT PREPARED FOR MY DREAM. WHO WOULD HAVE THOUGHT THAT SUCH A DREAM WOULD BE REALIZED WITHIN LOS ESTADOS UNIDOS?

150

ALTHOUGH THE LATINO MIDDLE CLASS BEGAN TO EXPAND IN THE EIGHTIES AND POLITICAL POWER AND PARTICIPATION WERE GAINED, GHETTO LIFE WAS THE ONLY LANDSCAPE FOR THE POOR.

VIVA - LA RAZA -

MI VIDA LOCA

WSB

QVOLE.

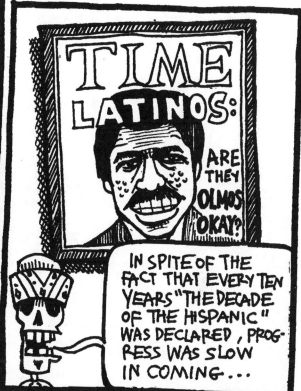

TIME

LATINOS:

ARE THEY OLMOS OKAY?

IN SPITE OF THE FACT THAT EVERY TEN YEARS "THE DECADE OF THE HISPANIC" WAS DECLARED, PROGRESS WAS SLOW IN COMING...

STILL, THE INFLUENCE OF LATINOS ON POP CULTURE GREW STRONGER. THE LOWRIDER CRAZE FLOURISHED. SOON, SALSA WOULD REPLACE KETCHUP AS THE BEST SELLING CONDIMENT.

ORALE CHUY !

LOWRIDER HOPPING CONTEST

CHEVY

RUFA = CEILING

MARKETA = SUPERMARKET

PARQUEAR = TO PARK

MOPEAR = TO MOP

FAXEAR = TO FAX

SOURCE: THE INSTITUTO OF SPANGLISH INSTITUTE

EVERYBODY BEGAN USING **SPANGLISH**!!!

SPANGLISH IS OFTEN PERCEIVED AS A DEROGATORY TERM. IT MEANS A WORD OR SENTENCE THAT IS PART IN SPANISH AND PART IN ENGLISH.

EDWARD JAMES OLMOS

THE MILAGRO BEANFIELD WAR

HOLLYWOOD BEGAN TO PRODUCE MOVIES FEATURING MORE HOPEFUL, POSITIVE, INTELLIGENT, AND WELL-ROUNDED HISPANIC CHARACTERS.

HE'S KIDDING RIGHT?

I WANT TO INSPIRE LATINOS, TO MAKE THEM SEEK A MEANINGFUL LIFE.

DOGS ALLOWED BUT NOT MEXICANS. ¡DISCULPE!

THE UNITED STATES TRIED TO CONTROL THE GREAT INFLUX OF IMMIGRANTS FROM SOUTH OF THE RIO GRANDE BY PASSING THE SIMPSON-MAZZOLI ACT AND SHORTLY AFTER IT, THE IMMIGRATION REFORM AND CONTROL ACT

THIS MEANT ENDLESS RAIDS DETENTIONS, DEPORTATIONS, AND BEATINGS...

WE'RE STILL TREATED WORSE THAN DOGS!

AND WE TAKE THE BAD JOBS, ALONG WITH THE GOOD BEATINGS...

WHEN WILL THE UNITED STATES REALIZE THAT IMMIGRATION IS A TWO-WAY STREET? UNLESS LATIN AMERICAN COUNTRIES INCREASE THEIR PER-CAPITA EARNING, THE DESIRE TO LOOK ELSEWHERE FOR A BETTER LIFE WILL CONTINUE. LIKEWISE, WITHOUT IMMIGRANTS WHERE WOULD THE ECONOMIES OF TEXAS, CALIFORNIA, ARIZONA AND NEW MEXICO BE?

TONITE
LIVE! IN CONCERT
THE MAMBO KINGS
PLAY SONGS OF LOVE
BACKED BY TITO
PUENTE AND CELIA CRUZ

SPECIAL APPEARANCE
BY
OSCAR
HIJUELOS
PULITZER
PRIZE
WINNER

IN 1989, OSCAR HIJUELOS, A CUBAN-AMERICAN NOVELIST, WAS AWARDED THE PULITZER PRIZE FOR HIS NOVEL, **THE MAMBO KINGS PLAY SONGS OF LOVE**. IT WAS THE FIRST TIME SUCH A PRESTIGIOUS AMERICAN LITERARY PRIZE WAS GIVEN TO A LATINO

SANDRA CISNEROS "HOUSE ON MANGO STREET"

JULIA ALVAREZ "HOW THE GARCIA GIRLS LOST THEIR ACCENTS"

"NECESSITY IS THE DAUGHTER OF INVENTION... OR IS IT ITS MOTHER?"

YOU HIGH-SPANICS CAN'T EVEN GET BENJAMIN FRANKLIN'S FAMOUS EXPRESSION CORRECT!

EL VIEJO LOCO JESSE HELMS

ALMOST IMMEDIATELY, THERE WAS A BOOM OF LATINA WRITERS. WOMEN DESCRIBED THEIR PLIGHT IN ELEGANT, MEMORABLE PROSE.

THE AGE OF AQUARIUS HAD ARRIVED! THE SOVIET EMPIRE COLLAPSED, THE BERLIN WALL CAME DOWN, AND IN THE UNITED STATES, LATINOS SEEMED CLOSER TO FINDING THEIR OWN VOICE THAN EVER BEFORE.

IN 1992, THE QUINCENTENNIAL OF COLUMBUS' VOYAGE TO THE NEW WORLD WAS CELEBRATED WORLDWIDE. A PUBLIC DEBATE ERUPTED: HAD THE SPANIARDS BEEN TOO VIOLENT IN THEIR ENTERPRISE ACROSS THE ATLANTIC? SHOULDN'T SUCH AN EVENT—THE ARRIVAL OF EUROPEANS TO THE AMERICAS—BE CONDEMNED?

ONE NIGHT ONLY / SOLO UNA NOCHE

CONCERT OF THE CENTURY!

LATINO POP STARS OF THE MILLENNIUM

GLORIA ESTEFAN
& MIAMI SOUND MACHINE

SELENA
LUIS MIGUEL

JUST ADDED

EL EX-MENUDO
RICKY MARTIN

LA EX-SELENA
JENNIFER LOPEZ

CRISTINA AGUILERA
Y LOS CALAVERA "ROC EN HUESPAÑOL"

TICKETS
$20.50

A
CROSSOVER
DREAMS
PRODUCTION

IN MEMORY
OF TITO
PUENTE

156

IN 1995, **SELENA**, THE POPULAR TEJANA SINGER, WAS IMMORTALIZED BY HER FANS. SHE WAS ASSASINATED BY A CRAZED EMPLOYEE, YOLANDA SALDIVAR.

HER TRAGIC DEATH PUSHED THE WHOLE NATION INTO A STATE OF SHOCK.

ONLY IN TRAGEDY, IT SEEMS, DOES THE WHOLE COUNTRY COME TOGETHER TO CELEBRATE HISPANIC CULTURE. OR AM I WRONG? IT ALSO HAPPENED WHEN RITCHIE VALENS WAS KILLED. OR WHEN GLORIA ESTEFAN, THE CUBAN MUSIC STAR, WAS INJURED IN A BUS ACCIDENT.

SCENE #1: "NAME RECOGNITION"

SCENE #2: "CAN'T BE WITH YOU, CAN'T BE WITHOUT YOU."

SCENE #3 "IMMORTALITY."

YOU'VE SHOWN US THE HISTORY OF LATINOS FROM 1542 TO THE PRESENT. THE MILLENNIUM IS COMING TO AN END. WHAT HAS CHANGED?

MMMM...

ARE LATINOS BETTER OFF? CAN ONE REALLY COMPILE A HISTORY OF LATINOS AS A SINGLE, HOMOGENIZED GROUP? WOULDN'T WE BE BETTER TO APPROACH EACH OF THE SUBGROUPS - CHICANOS, PUERTO RICANS, CUBAN-AMERICANS - AS SELF-SUFFICIENT, INDEPENDENT POPULATIONS?

YOU TELL ME. SIMPLY LOOK AROUND...

WELL, MUCH HAS CHANGED. AS A MINORITY GROUP, LATINOS ARE MORE HOMOGENIZED THAN EVER. BUT THERE IS STILL TENSION AMONG THE VARIOUS GROUPS, NO DOUBT ABOUT IT.

AND YET, ALL PRETTY MUCH SPEAK THE SAME LANGUAGE, WATCH THE SAME TV SHOWS, DANCE TO THE SAME MUSIC...

U.S. Population

Latinos by Race
Mestizo: a lot
Black: not so many
White: not so many
Other: few

Latinos by Religion
Catholic: a lot
Protestant: many
Jewish: very few
Other: many

azteca.net   hisp.com
latinolink.com
pocho.com
hopscotch.org
coqui.net
latinoweb.com
mercado.com
generation
mex.com
jibaros.com
lacucaracha.com
aztlannet.net
brownpride.com
yupi.com latinola.com
reconquista.com
raza.org azteca.net
hisp.com pocho.com
hopscotch.org

THE RIO GRANDE IS STILL THE DIVIDING LINE, THE END AND THE BEGINNING. BUT TODAY'S BORDERS ARE ONLY IMAGINARY, BECAUSE TELECOMMUNICATIONS AND FREE TRADE MAKE US ALL PART OF A SINGLE TRIBE.

THIS VIEW, OF COURSE, HAS ITS TRAPS!

163

FIN

ACKNOWLEDGMENTS

My wholehearted gratitude to the many people who in one way or another helped while this book was taking shape. In naming them all I run the risk of inexcusable omission. But a handful stand out. Edna Acosta Belen, Harold Augenbraum, Antonio Benitez-Rojo, Ariel Dorfman, Don Fehr, Felipe Galindo, Maria Herrera Sobek, Rolando Hinojosa-Smith, Jill Kneerim, Himilce Novas, Gustavo Perez-Firmat, Abraham Stavans, Virgil Suarez, and Gerardo Villacres affected the content with their ideas and conversations. The people at the Institute of Latin American Studies at the University of London, where I was Visiting Research Fellow in 1998—99, as well as my British friend Anthony Rudolf, stood by undefeated while faxes and Fedexes went back and forth. And the staff of *Hopscotch: A Cultural Review*, at Amherst, Massachusetts, and Durham, North Carolina, especially Melissa Lorenzo, were invariably on the line wherever I found myself, if in Spain, London, New York, Berkeley, or Los Angeles. Sheila Friedling, formerly at Holmes and Meier and currently at The Jewish Museum of New York, thought of the idea first. Philip Lief nurtured it from the beginning and brought it to light. Linda Perrin guided me through a labyrinth of my own creation, Jamie Saxon brought light into the pages and orchestrated transatlantic communications, and Mercedes Anderson proofread it with a sharp eye. Don Fehr at Basic Books was a patient, encouraging in-house editor and an excellent friend, and John Kemmerer, his assistant, was *siempre listo*. My beloved Alison Sparks commented wisely at every stage of the creative and editorial process, and—in spite of their young ages—so did my children, Joshua and Isaiah. And of course, Lalo Lopez Alcaraz, who poured in his heart, time, and ink in equal measure. Lalo wishes to thank his lovely Chicana schoolteacher- wife, Victoria, for being the visual inspiration for Maestra, and their baby daughter Amaya for waking him up every morning at 730 a.m. without fail. He is also indebted to all the cartoonists, illustrators, and photographers whose visual material was the basis for many of the cartoons in this book.

The general sources I relied on directly or otherwise—historical, sociological, cultural, and literary—are countless. A complete list appears on pages 215—229 of my book *The Hispanic Condition: Reflections on Culture and Identity in America* (New York, 1996) and, in expanded, updated form, on pages 267—293 of the book's Spanish translation, *La condición hispánica* (Mexico, 1999).

The specific quotes and graphics I used come from, in order of appearance: *Castaways*, by Alvar Núñez Cabeza de Vaca, edited by Enrique Pupo-Walker (Los Angeles, 1993); Gaspar Pérez de Villagrá, *The History of New Mexico* (Albuquerque, 1992); the edict of May 26, 1570, *Historical Documents Relating to New Mexico, Nueva Viscaya, and Approaches Thereto, to 1773* (Washington, DC,

1923); Fray Bartolomé de Las Casas, *Very Brief Account of the Destruction of the Indies* (New York, 1909); Padre Junípero Serra, *Writings of Junípero Serra* (Washington, DC, 1955); General Scott's account of the *Battle of Puebla, Chronicles of the Gringos: The U.S. Army in the Mexican War, 1846—1848, Accounts of Eyewitnesses and Combatants,* edited by George Winston Smith and Charles Judah (Albuquerque, 1968); a Mexican account of the Alamo, "A Critical Study of the Siege of the Alamo and of the Personnel of Its Defenders," by Amelia Williams, *Southwestern Historical Quarterly* (July 1933); Daniel Cosmo Villegas, *American Extremes,* trans., Americo Paredes (Austin, TX, 1969); "The Ballad of Gregorio Cortez," from *With His Pistol in His Hand: A Border Ballad and Its Hero,* by Americo Paredes (Austin, TX, 1958); "Spain's Sense of Justice," by C. G. Bush, *Latin America in Caricature,* by John J. Johnson (Austin, TX, 1980); exchange between senior students and Charles Francis Adams at the University of Wisconsin, 1897, *The Mirror of War: American Society and the Spanish-American War,* by Gerald F. Linderman (Ann Arbor, MI, 1974); "The Cuban Melodrama," by C.J. Taylor, *Latin America in Caricature;* "Abandoned," by F.I. Richards, *Latin America in Caricature;* "The Cavalry at Santiago," *The Rough Riders,* by Theodore Roosevelt (New York, 1990); Miguel Antonio Otero's speech, *My Nine Years as Governor of the Territory of New Mexico* (Albuquerque, 1940); "To Columbus," by Rubén Darío, *Imagining Columbus: The Literary Voyage,* by Ilan Stavans (New York, 1993); "Two Cubas," by José Martí, *The Hispanic Condition* (New York, 1995); "La Guera," from *500 Años del Pueblo Chicano* (Albuquerque, 1991); Bernardo Vega, *Memoirs of Bernardo Vega* (New York, 1984); "To the Prosecuted," by José de Diego, trans. by Roberto Santiago, *Boricuas: Influential Puerto Rican Writings—An Anthology,* edited by Roberto Santiago (New York, 1995); Speech of 1936 by Pedro Albizu Campos, translated by Roberto Santiago; "On Recent Disturbances in Puerto Rico," by Luis Muñoz Marín, *Boricuas: Influential Puerto Rican Writing—An Anthology,* edited by Roberto Santiago; "To Elsie," by William Carlos Williams, *The Collected Poems of William Carlos Williams: vol. I: 1909—1939* (New York, 1987); *The Los Angeles Daily News,* from *Occupied America: A History of Chicanos,* by Rodolfo Acuña (3rd edition, New York, 1988); quote from Octavio Paz, *The Labyrinth of Solitude,* by Octavio Paz (New York, 1961); Rodolfo "Corky" Gonzáles, *Yo soy Joaquín/I Am Joaquín,* by Rodolfo "Corky" Gonzáles (New York, 1967); speech by The Raza Unida Party leader, *Youth, Identity, Power: The Chicano Movement,* by Carlos Muñoz, Jr. (London and New York, 1989); "La tierra se llama Juan," by Pablo Neruda, *Selected Poems of Pablo Neruda* (New York, 1983); Oscar "Zeta" Acosta, *The Autobiography of a Brown Buffalo,* (San Francisco, 1972); "Who Is a Chicano? And What Is It the Chicanos Want?," by Rubén Salazar, *Border Correspondent: Selected Writings, 1955—1970,* by Rubén Salazar, edited by Mario T. Garcia (Los Angeles, 1995).

INDEX